HALL OF FAME

Tom Blair

ARTHUR H. STOCKWELL LTD
Torrs Park   Ilfracombe   Devon
Established 1898
www.ahstockwell.co.uk

British Library Cataloguing-in-Publication Data.
A catalogue record for this book is available
from the British Library.

Arthur H. Stockwell Ltd bears no responsibility
for the accuracy of information recorded in this book.

ISBN 978-0-7223-4027-1
Printed in Great Britain by
Arthur H. Stockwell Ltd
Torrs Park   Ilfracombe
Devon

FOREWORD

My name is Tom Blair. I have never written anything longer than a letter in my life and do not profess to be an author.

Meeting John Hall, and talking to this handicapped young man, has been one of the most humbling experiences of my life.

John mentioned that he would like to write his life story and try to relate what it is like to be severely handicapped, but he felt that he was not equipped to do so.

This was back in July 1992. For five years we sat together when we both had a bit of spare time, John telling his stories and me attempting to capture the interesting bits on paper.

The man's determination, guts and sheer will power have at times made me feel quite inadequate.

Here is your story, John, as told by you and as I interpret it. I am proud to know you and even more proud to say I am your friend.

Tom Blair

CHAPTER I

CHILDHOOD

This is my story, dedicated to my mum, June Richardson Hall, and my dad, John Pearson Hall. I was born on 31 July 1955, so I was thirty-seven years old in July 1992, when this writing commenced.

During pregnancy, my mother developed German measles and consequently complications set in. I was born prematurely, weighing in at a fabulous 2 lb – the same as a bag of sugar. The gynaecologist did not hold out much hope for me, and Mum and Dad prepared for the worst, but even as a baby my determination to survive was there in the heart that would serve me throughout my life. From the start I had the driving force that, in later years, seemed to say, "You can do it, you can do it."

I was nearly two years old before the extent of my disability was fully realised. Not only was I severely physically handicapped and couldn't walk or run properly, but I was also deaf. Communication was impossible. The official name of my condition is 'spasticity, affecting co-ordination of legs, and deafness'. Of course, as far as I was concerned, I was normal; others were just different to me. They moved differently and they made funny muffled sounds when they opened their mouths. They pointed at me a lot, laughed and ran away, making even more funny, muffled noises.

I didn't understand why.

I was between three and four years old when I really started to pull myself up and use the furniture as props to get from A to B. The exercise gradually made me stronger, and one day, much to my parents' surprise, they found me at the edge of the road with traffic whizzing past. They called, "John, John," but of course I couldn't hear them. Not only that, but I couldn't hear the traffic either. There was only a strange muffled sound. I knew no fear.

My deafness meant that I could not understand what was being said to me, and of course I was not learning as I should have done. I did not understand all of this at the time and was quite happy in my own slow-moving, practically silent, muffled world.

Mum was a very beautiful lady, and she and Dad were very good to me.

I remember vividly being doubled up with pain and writhing in agony one day, and once again my poor mum was thrown into the pits of worry and anxiety.

"Could it be food poisoning? Has he picked something up?"

I couldn't tell them. I was rushed to hospital, where I underwent emergency surgery for acute appendicitis – one more narrow escape. By this time I was about four years old.

Time went by and my parents thought about school – what to do?

One morning, I was bathed and dressed, my hair was brushed and combed, and I was taken to the village playschool. Why did the other children all stop playing and point and look?

They looked happy because they were laughing, but I didn't realise they were laughing *at* me – my legs and the way I walked and tried to communicate. The more I tried to communicate, the more they laughed and pointed, poking me, making fun and running away despite the teachers' remonstrations. My handicap prevented any two-way communication. I found myself in an impossible position, unable to take part in day-to-day learning, or to fathom out the intricacies of the strange rituals the others seemed to be continuously engaged in.

I now know that they were simple games, but to take part one had to be able to run and hear what was going on. I just sat there, looking on.

Another playschool was recommended. It was thought that more individual attention could be given, because there were fewer children, but this also proved fruitless. It simply meant fewer children pointing, laughing and making fun of me. It was soon realised that I had special needs, and, if I were to learn anything at all, something drastic would have to be done. Advice was sought.

The local authority recommended that I be taken to a special school for the deaf and disabled. I knew nothing of this decision at this stage; I was only four and a half years old and could not understand that it was all for my own good.

What a predicament for my darling mother and my father! How were they to tell me I was going to have to go into a special home?

Here is how they went about it:

They knew I loved my grandparents, and I was told that soon I would be taken to see them for a holiday.

They lived in Peterborough, and Mum and Dad somehow communicated to me that we would be going in a car and that Nanna and Granpa were waiting for me. I remember being very excited indeed, and I couldn't wait to get in the car.

The big day came. I was bathed and dressed – white shirt, bow tie, black suit, gleaming polished shoes. My case was packed with my pyjamas, clean underwear, slippers and a few precious toys.

I could never remember having so many sweets and so many cuddles and kisses from Mum. This was great. I remember the Fruit Chews to this day. They were lovely. They certainly knew how to keep me pacified, and of course there was Nanna and Granpa to look forward to. Even more spoiling when I got there! Or so I thought.

The time came to leave and the car was outside. I think it was an old Morris. It had spoked wheels and a lovely smell of polished leather. Dad lifted my little case and, nodding, held out his hand towards the door. Mum bent down. She smelled lovely. She hugged and kissed me, straightened my clothes and kissed me again. She looked very sad, but I didn't know why at the time.

I now know that when I left she must have been broken-hearted.

The car started. I was in the back seat and Mum's tearful face filled the window. I waved and waved until we turned the corner and I could no longer see her.

Dad's friend was driving and Dad was sitting in the front. I remember the mudguards and the funny door handles. I'm sure it was a Morris.

We drove for what seemed ages. Then the car pulled into a driveway. The house belonged to someone Dad knew. We had tea – I had boiled eggs and toasted soldiers, followed by fruit cake. It was a beautiful warm day; the sun was shining. As we prepared to leave, the lady put a boiled egg in a box for me to take with me. I didn't understand this and still don't to this day. Maybe she thought I would get hungry on the way, or maybe she thought they would starve me where I was going. Who knows?

We were on our way again and it felt like a magic journey. The countryside was beautiful – cows, sheep, fields, trees, houses and villages. I was fascinated by it all, and I was completely unaware of the real reason for our journey.

Dad kept turning round, his lips moving. He spoke to me, patting me on the knee and comforting me, smiling, reassuring. I could not understand it at all.

The journey lasted a long time; I was getting tired and less enchanted as time went by. I thought of Nanna and Granpa and the welcome supper and bed that was waiting for us.

The car turned, and I saw a very high, long stone wall. We drove through a big black gate. On each side were two stone pillars; on top of them were large stone balls. I was becoming anxious and confused. There was a house on the right inside the gate – the caretaker's. The drive seemed endless. I looked out of the car window and saw a big clock and, to my left, what I thought was a tunnel. This turned out to be an archway.

The car jerked to a stop outside a large house. I remember thinking, 'Nanna and Granpa must be important.' Dad lifted me out of the car and put me on my feet. As we moved towards the house, Dad held my hand. I had difficulty in placing one leg in front of the other, but I can never remember pain as such, except when I kept stumbling and bruising and cutting the same vulnerable spots. I did cry a lot because I was always stumbling and hurting the same areas, although they used to bandage these places to try to protect them.

I could see a lot of children's faces at the windows as we walked towards the massive door.

Dad pushed the doorbell. He was still holding me by the other hand. 'Bing-Bong-Bing.' I learned later that this was the noise the doorbell made when you pushed the button.

A lady came to the door. We walked through an inner porchway and were taken into the school office. I wondered, 'Where's Nanna and Granpa?'

The lady and Dad talked for what seemed ages about my future and what would be best for me.

I was looking around and I remember large pictures on the wall. The floors were gleaming; you could see your reflection. It looked very posh indeed, but where were Nanna and Granpa? I was confused. I tugged at Dad's jacket and tried to make him understand. He made several gestures to tell me he was talking to the lady and to be quiet.

I watched a number of children walking by, and they all seemed funny. Some walked funny, some had big heads and were twisted and bent into strange shapes. Some had faces like the masks we used to buy in the shop and deformed hands. Most of them had peculiar objects dangling out of their ears. I was becoming more and more agitated – and where were Nanna and Granpa?

I held on tightly to Dad's trouser leg. He bent down and cuddled me, hugged me tight and kissed me. I could see tears welling up in his eyes as he handed me to the lady. I didn't understand what was happening. I tried to break away. I kicked, I pinched, and I fought to get away and run after my Dad.

'Oh, Dad, how could you leave me here with all these strange people!'

I cried, 'Dad! Dad!'

The lady tried to console me, but finally she had to smack me to control my hysteria. Apparently Dad cried all the way home. He wanted to come and get me, but he was persuaded not to and that it would be for the best.

My heart was still breaking.

The lady offered me a sweet; she then gave me a toy. I remember it was quite heavy, and in sheer temper I heaved it and it crashed through a very large window. Everyone panicked and ran. I was smacked hard on the bottom – very, very hard.

'Dad! Dad! Dad!' I cried and cried for hours.

Eventually I calmed down and was taken to tea. I cannot remember what it was – my young mind was in turmoil.

I was taken upstairs to the bedroom. The stairs were very wide; they looked enormous, and I was not yet five years old.

I was undressed, bathed and made ready for bed. Then I was given a purple dressing gown with a cord and tassels, and some new slippers. One of the teachers undid the cord, slipped my dressing gown off and lifted me into bed. It was a small bed and I had a little locker at the side for my things. There were eight other boys in the room with me, all severely physically handicapped and deaf. We were all about five years old.

The lights were switched off, and I remember a dim red light which shone all night. I was still crying and crying and crying.

'Where's my Dad? Where's Granpa and Nanna?'

I was frightened and anxious. I thought of my beautiful mother and fell asleep, sobbing.

I was shaken awake the following morning. My eyes were red-raw and sore from crying myself to sleep.

The housemother looked a kind lady, but she was very strict. She helped to wash me then get me dressed in my new school uniform. I remember it clearly: a grey shirt, yellow and green tie, grey trousers held up by a yellow and grey snake-clasp belt, grey jacket, long grey stockings with green-striped tops, a grey jacket with the Rayners School badge and a school cap with the same badge. My black shoes were highly polished by my housemother. I felt very posh and very smart. The uniform was worn every day except Saturday; we even wore it for church parade on Sunday.

I had been to see a Mr Willen, to be fitted with a hearing aid. This, of course, confused me even more. I was suddenly hearing noises I had never heard clearly before, such as laughing, crying, shouting and talking. I also remember the hearing aid hurting me sometimes, tremendously. Later I learned that the pain was caused by something to do with the ambient air pressure.

So, here I was, not yet five years old, left in an institution and ready to start my first day.

My room-mates and I were marched to the dining hall for breakfast. I still remember what it was: cornflakes and milk, scrambled egg and toast with a mug of tea – and, oh yes, I wore an apron covering my new suit in case I made a mess. The food was lovely and there was plenty of it. Yes, we were well fed.

Before meals we all had to stand and say a prayer. I did not really understand what was going on; I just watched everyone else and copied what they did. After the meal, we were signalled to stand again and put our hands together and give thanks to the Lord for our meal.

By this time I was beginning to realise that Nanna and Granpa were not there and never would be. The whole thing was like a nightmare and I was terribly homesick for Mum and Dad. In my childish way, I thought they had deserted me and didn't want me.

We were lined up once again outside the dining room and marched to the gym for our first assembly. The youngest and smallest were seated at the front. We were told to sit with our arms folded and our housemother indicated by pressing her fingers to her lips that we had to be quiet. Our next signal was to all stand. This heralded the arrival of Mr Brout, the headmaster. He was very tall and thin with spectacles on the point of his nose. He wore a black three-piece suit and a white shirt, and he smoked a pipe.

I was to learn later that he was a disciplinarian and worked strictly to the book.

He made his way to the front of the gym with Mr Evans, who played the piano whilst Mr Brout pointed to the large song poster.

We attempted to sing 'Jesus Loves Me, Yes I know'.

With the majority having some form of speech impediment, we never would make the Albert Hall. The headmaster and Mr Evans could be heard above everyone else; they had very strong voices indeed, as I was to learn on more than one occasion.

When assembly was over we were then marched off to our various classrooms, which were marvellous havens with sandpits and boxes of toys – we played all day, but of course we were learning as well. I remember the teachers, Miss Dennis and Miss Gouder, well. They used sign language, which I did not understand but would gradually get to learn.

There were two classrooms with interconnecting doors. The other room was for the girls, who, at this stage, I thought were very peculiar beings indeed. I remember one girl, Lesley, who had a steel support fitted from her foot to her hip. Even at that tender age she had to use a walking stick to hobble about. Both her legs were badly scarred due to surgery. She was also partially deaf.

Being in a place like Rayners School makes you realise that there is always someone worse off than yourself. Young Graham Watford, for example, was terribly deformed. He looked as though he came from another planet. He could not speak at all, was totally deaf and could hardly get around. Compared to poor old Graham, I was a film star. My age group also included some very pretty girls, but all of them were deformed in some way, with speech impediments, deafness and mobility problems.

For about six months we played with sand and toys; and all the while, without realising it, we were gradually being introduced to sign language and speech therapy. I realise now that our teachers were highly skilled therapists.

The first thing I learnt to say in sign language was "Good morning." Can you imagine not only having to learn how to speak but also how to translate each word into a sign? It was quite a task for a five-and-a-half-year-old. I was still convinced that I had been abandoned by everyone, including my parents. They had tricked me into coming to Rayners School and, although the teachers did everything possible to entertain me and fill my days, I was very lonely and very sad for a long time. Also I seemed to get into a lot of trouble.

One day, we were playing in the sandpit and the girls were all wearing nice dresses. We started throwing sand and generally fooling around, and I thought it was a great idea to pour some sand from a bucket inside a girl's dress. The teacher had other thoughts!

I was dragged, by the ears, to the headmaster. I was

about to find out what a disciplinarian he was. All my classmates were assembled, my trousers and pants were pulled down, and I was smacked very hard on the bottom. I wet myself with fear. I pulled up my trousers and ran to my bedroom and tried to hide in my bed. I cried for what seemed ages.

I had never been smacked so hard, and I will never forget the utter humiliation.

Eventually a teacher came and calmed me down. I was taken to the surgery and had cold cream applied to my still-smarting bottom.

On returning to the classroom, everyone was unusually quiet. Sign language was used to spread the message that anyone behaving in a similar manner could expect similar treatment.

Of course, there were good times. At Halloween we all dressed up and had great fun, and on the Fifth of November we had toffee apples, hot dogs, beefburgers, fireworks, a bonfire, rockets and sparklers. One year a sparkler burned my hand, and once again I was slipped off to first aid to have treatment. It wasn't too bad, though, and I was quickly back on the scene, learning all about Guy Fawkes.

By the time I was about six years old I was picking up sign language quickly; and, thanks to my hearing aid, the words were coming thick and fast. Although I did not realise it at the time, for me, life was really just beginning. At last I was learning to communicate. However, my vocal chords were still a stumbling block, and I found great difficulty in forming my words. This, of course, all added to my frustration. I knew what I wanted to say, but the words just wouldn't come out.

Can you imagine forming a picture in your mind about what you want to say, opening your mouth and all that comes out is a garbled jumble of noise?

I soon found ways of making myself understood, though. I would simplify big words like *impossible* to "Can't do it." I adjusted the language to suit myself and my impediment. I invented a sort of John Hall-ese, which adjusted English language to my word power.

Now that I was communicating, albeit in my own

fashion, I was starting to learn even more. I began to live. Things began to make sense; I could now understand what people were saying. Then there was sign language, and I simultaneously began lip-reading very effectively. Life was becoming a whole new ball game.

At this time, possibly due to that fact that I had begun to understand my surroundings and, in my childish way, was starting to enjoy the learning cycle, I began to calm down. I had fewer frustration-based temper tantrums and was less of a problem to my teachers and tutors.

The hearing aid helped me to 'listen to myself', and gradually my own speech, although by no means perfect, began to improve. Can you imagine how it felt to hear, for the first time, the springtime birds singing so beautifully in the trees and the happy sounds of other children laughing, singing and playing. At first I was in a trance-like state, so enthralled was I by it all. I suppose, in a way, I was very lucky. So-called 'normal' people take all of this for granted. I was nearly seven years old when I first heard the birds sing!

At this time, I was beginning to understand the problems of the other children – their deformities, deafness and speech impediments.

During all this time Mum kept in contact by writing and sending parcels, but Dad never corresponded in any way. Mum used to say he sent his love. He was a merchant seaman, and perhaps he was too busy to write.

It was 1962 and we were all now looking forward to Christmas holidays; for me this meant getting home to Mum. But before this we had the school Christmas party to look forward to. I remember being very, very excited. We were all dressed in our best uniforms and polished shoes and we assembled in the dining room, which was decorated. There was a huge Christmas tree with an angel on top.

Routine seating arrangements were forgotten, and we could choose to sit with our special friends. I remember my friends so clearly: Judanka, Christine, Julie, Kevin, Paul, Michael and Clive. We all sat together.

Judanka was only partially deaf and could speak very well. She also had no physical disability.

Christine was deaf with a speech impediment, and Julie was the same.

Dear old Kevin was very outgoing, but at any time, and without warning, he could be stricken with the most horrendous epileptic fit.

Paul was completely deaf. He could speak very little but was always getting into trouble. He was very mischievous.

Michael was very tall, well spoken, intelligent and partially deaf.

As in most groups, we had the party clown – Clive. He was always making people laugh and taking the mickey. He was stone deaf and all his jokes were in sign language. His arms and hands used to whirl like a windmill. We had to be quick; otherwise we would miss the punchline or 'punch sign'.

The Christmas dinner was scrumptious: chicken or turkey, roast potatoes and all the trimmings, Christmas pudding and custard, lemonade, coke, crackers and, of course, the funny hats.

The prayers were said, both before (Thank you for providing, Lord) and after (Thank you for your love and care, Lord). Then we were all assembled in the gym, the lights were dimmed and the Christmas-tree lights were turned on. It really was beautiful, and I realise now what a tremendous effort the staff must have put in to make the occasion so festive.

The lights flashed and we were told that Father Christmas was on his way. He appeared in the doorway. Everyone cheered and shouted. This is where the hearing aid is handy: at least you can turn it down – or off, come to that.

"Ho! Ho! Ho!" he bellowed. "Merry Christmas! Ho! Ho! Ho!"

He lowered his massive sack to the floor, sat down and started to call out our names.

When my turn came, I tried to peer beyond the beard, but to no avail. I did not know who it was.

My hand was duly shaken and I was given a parcel. I sped back to my friends and eagerly unwrapped it – a model car with people painted on the side and a friction-driven motor (the kind where you rub the wheels on the ground and then let go). We were also given an apple, a banana and some sweets.

I was still confused about Father Christmas, though, and I debated this with my friends.

Why was he covered in snow when it wasn't snowing?

How did he know everyone's name?

How did he manage to carry all the multitude of toys, apples, bananas and sweets?

"Who cares anyway?" said one friend.

It had all been lovely and now it was time for games, including oranges and lemons, musical chairs (difficult with some more deaf than others, but it is amazing how we managed), pin the tail on the donkey, blind man's buff and musical statues (very awkward, especially for those who had difficulty standing still at the best of times). The evening concluded with an Elvis Presley film. Some were asleep before the end of the film – no offence, Elvis!

We were all absolutely exhausted. We had had such a wonderful, marvellous time, but now I was looking forward to seeing Mum for Christmas.

Two or three days later we were all so excited when we were wakened and told to prepare for going home for the Christmas break. We put on our best suits and polished shoes, had our breakfast, brushed our teeth, and collected our cases, packed the previous night. We then waited in the assembly hall for the arrival of the bus that was to take us to Beaconsfield Station. This was all new and strange to me so, as you can imagine, it seemed like a marvellous adventure.

We all got off the coach and lined up, waiting for the steam engine pulling the train. I can see it now – an enormous black giant, belching and puffing smoke and steam everywhere. It rolled in and stopped, the doors opened and we were told to board the carriages. This was all carried out with a somewhat military precision. I remember the inside of the carriage – the old-fashioned lampshades; baggage nets, where we put our small cases; hot steam pipes under the seats; pictures on the wall, with a mirror in the middle; and the peculiar sooty smell that permeated the air. The door to the corridor was a sliding door.

It was all very exciting. If we wanted to go to the toilet we had to ask permission and be escorted by one of the teachers. I will never forget when I pulled the chain. I looked straight down through a hole, and the 'clickety-clack, clickety-clack' was louder. Needless to say, I pulled the chain a couple of times more than was required, just to hear this amplified 'clickety-clack, clickety-clack'.

I was one of the lucky ones with a seat by the window, and I could watch the countryside and all its wonders as we sped along. The trees were bare – asleep for the winter – and the cattle and horses stood in the fields with their heads lowered, looking terribly sad. I remember thinking how lucky we were to be in a snug warm carriage.

As with all school outings, there was a great deal of to-ing and fro-ing from carriage to carriage, and our teachers became terribly frustrated as they tried to control us. We had all the usual boredom-breakers like ludo, and snakes and ladders. I was caught cheating and was chastised by our minder.

At last, the train chugged to a stop at Marylebone Station, and we descended to the platform. We were told to line up, each of us holding a case in one hand and the hand of whoever stood next to us in the other. I remember being marched, as best we could (because, don't forget, most of us were physically disabled) to the Underground station, where we boarded a train for Waterloo.

On reaching Waterloo Station, the disembarking procedure was carried out again – the lining-up, holding hands and marching, marching, marching towards the massive grey building which was rumoured to be where our parents were waiting for us.

It had been three long months since I had seen Mum, and I wondered if she would be as excited as I was. After what seemed like endless flights of stairs, we came into this large room. I did not recognise Mum at first, but she recognised me. As she walked towards me I realised it was her.

She picked me up and my case fell from my hand. I thought she was going to squeeze the life out of me. I will never forget the hugs, the tears, the kisses, the warm glow and the flow of love between us – the pure undemanding warmth and love between a mother and her son. This is one of the happiest, fondest memories I have. I realised then that Mum did love me and had sent me away to grow and learn. Like most mothers, she had done what was best for her son, regardless of her feelings.

This was living. Mum took me shopping in London before we went to Waterloo Station to catch another steam train to Andover. If I remember correctly, it was 21 December when we arrived at 46 Perham Crescent, Ludgershall.

I went straight upstairs, took off my good school clothes and got into my old clothes for playing. My brother, Robert, was there and so was my baby sister, Gail. She was about two years old. Oh, it was lovely to be home!

Mum had already decorated the house for Christmas. There was a real Christmas tree with beautiful lights and a fairy on the top. The best surprise was that Dad had arrived home from the merchant navy, and I'll never forget his hugs and kisses and the feeling of being wanted.

Dad always brought home exotic, unusual presents from abroad – massive seashells and coral – and his stories were mind-boggling. Of course, now I was beginning to understand what he was saying. It was all so fascinating.

Christmas Eve came and all the presents were placed around the tree ready for Christmas morning. Mum and Dad were not well off, but somehow they always managed to get something for everyone. I remember that year I got a toy metal bus with the driver and passengers painted on the sides. I often wish I had kept those old toys – they would be worth something now.

Boxing Day was spent with Nanny and Grandad Hall, my Dad's parents. Oh, the scrumptious Christmas dinners, the black-and-white television, and the record player belting out the old favourites!

As in most families, my brother and I used to end up fighting and arguing, and this always culminated in us both being chastised. Our bottoms were smacked and we were sent to bed. Merry Christmas!

Robert used to mock me quite a bit – especially about the way I used to speak and the awkward way I walked. This of course made me very angry, and I used to attack him when I thought Mum and Dad weren't looking. Unfortunately I usually got nabbed and it all ended in tears again; but, despite all this, there was a deep bond and love between my brother and myself.

About this time I began to realise that all was not quite as it should be between Mum and Dad, but that is another story and not one that I want to dwell upon at this time.

The holiday was taken up with getting into mischief, being caught, having bottoms smacked, being sent to bed, getting hugs and kisses, and being told to be good. Soon it was time to pack the little case, and Mum and Dad took me back to the meeting place at Marylebone. I remember Dad saying goodbye at home and lifting me up and holding me in his strong arms.

"Don't forget, Daddy loves you," he said. "God bless you and goodbye."

Andover Station did not look quite so inviting this time. I knew that when we arrived in London, Mum would also be saying goodbye. I felt depressed. I did not know at the time that this would be the last time I would see my father. It was Christmas 1962; I was seven years old.

Back at school, it took two or three days to settle in after the holiday. The teachers knew this and were very patient. We were moved to a new room because of new entrants, and we all soon got down to the business of learning again. Lessons, discipline and making friends went on pretty much as before.

Easter came and went, more or less like Christmas: packing, being taken to the station, getting on the train, getting off the train, marching to the grey building, meeting Mum and going home, fighting with my brother, making up, and eventually going back. Except that Dad wasn't there this time, life was now becoming routine.

I used to get a letter from home about every two weeks or so, and as we weren't able to read very well at this stage the teacher used to read our letters out to us in class.

One particular letter arrived in early June 1963, and it was one I'll never forget as long as I live. The teacher opened the envelope, unfolded the letter and read it. She went very quiet for a moment, but decided to read on. She informed me that my father had died at sea. Of course I was stunned, but I did not quite understand at the time. In later years I discovered that there had been an article in the local newspaper which read:

> Mrs J. Hall of Perham Crescent, Ludgershall, heard yesterday that her merchant-seaman husband, John Pearson, aged thirty-three years, died in Port of Spain as a result of an accident. The cause of death was asphyxia.

It was now summer, and time once again to pack up the little case and prepare for the journey home.

My impediments were still causing problems. Other children still made fun of me – the way I talked, the way I walked and so on. This distressed me at home during the summer holiday.

They were long, lonely days. My brother had his own friends and I spent a lot of time by myself. There were some times when other children would allow me to play with them, and I treasured these times when I would feel part of the gang, but inevitably they would lose patience because they could not understand what I was saying. Soon I would find myself alone again, having to amuse myself.

I was now beginning to realise that I was happier at school. I did not feel out of place there. I now thought of school as home, and home as somewhere to spend the holidays.

The death of my father affected me more than I understood at the time. I withdrew into myself and tried to come to terms with the fact that I would never see him again. It was too much for me to fully comprehend. I was only eight years old.

The years now flew past: 1964, 1965, 1966, 1967, 1968 and 1969 were all pretty much the same. Activities, routines, learning, school holidays, back and forward – all these things followed the same pattern. But in 1970 there were some dramatic changes. I was now reaching puberty and maturing fast. I was becoming more and more concerned about my disabilities. I was also apprehensive about my academic ability in reading and writing, and mathematics was a complete mystery to me.

I was still looking forward and was optimistic about leaving school. I knew I had a long way to go and I was a late developer. I realised that I had an enormous task ahead of me with my education.

I knew within myself that very soon I would be thrust into the cold real world, away from the security of school, the friendship of my peers and the care and understanding of my tutors.

I also accepted that on that beautiful day when Dad had taken me on the car journey to see Nanna and Granpa the best decision had been made for me.

God bless you, Dad. Rest in peace. I love you and will miss you always.

My friends at school were like brothers and sisters to me, and this made the thought of leaving them more and more difficult as the time approached.

I remember I had terrible mixed feelings of excitement, trepidation, joy and sadness, all happening at once.

I had started to notice girls! Many of my immediate friends were of the opposite sex, and I was very fond of one or two of them. In the final rush to get things together in preparation for leaving we forgot to exchange addresses or anything else, and to this day I have not contacted any of them. I often think of them, though, on that last day – the hugs, the tears and the fond farewells, some in sign language.

Before we knew what was happening, we were boarding the bus and heading towards the station, just as had happened so many times before. This journey was much the same, except that this was the last trip we would ever take from Rayners School.

Anyway I had six weeks' summer holiday to look forward to – and my birthday. I would be sixteen years old on 31 July.

CHAPTER II

COURT GRANGE

Apart from the trauma of growing up, with the trials and tribulations of puberty, I was really worried about what the future held for me. I knew within myself that I had a long hard road ahead of me if I wanted to develop further and be self-sufficient.

With all of this in my head, we eventually arrived at good old 46 Perham Crescent, Ludgershall – home sweet home. I was home to stay, or that is what I thought.

It was a lovely feeling – plenty of hugs from my brother and sister. I really felt wanted and secure.

Eventually we discussed my future. Imagine my feelings when my mother read a letter from social services stating that they had found a place for me in another training establishment: Court Grange near Newton Abbot.

There was I, expecting six weeks at home, only to realise that in just over a fortnight I would be in a completely different environment, meeting completely new people.

This move could have caused many problems financially, but fortunately my father had left money in trust for me. I was not supposed to be able to use or touch the capital until I was eighteen, but the court granted my mother permission to draw £500 to kit me out. All of my previous uniform, down to underwear and socks and shoes, had to be parcelled up and returned to Rayners School. This was done.

The requirements of Court Grange included not only daywear but also pyjamas, dressing gowns, slippers and work clothes. Another problem at this time was my rapid growth rate. Anyway, everything I required was purchased, even down to new suitcases, and I was prepared for my next but not quite so traumatic move.

At least I knew where I was going this time, and I was slightly more confident. I could communicate to a degree, and my apprehension was cushioned by excitement and curiosity.

The day arrived to depart to Newton Abbot and thence to Court Grange. It was early August 1970. The train arrived at our destination and Mum and I boarded a taxi. Eventually we reached a gate and the taxi turned into a narrow road lined with trees. I remember the large fields and realised we were in the countryside.

Court Grange came into view. It reminded me of a Bavarian castle with battlements and towers, and I was to learn later that there were many strange tales connected with the building. I must admit I was a bit frightened. I had been watching some Frankenstein-type horror films and this place just fitted the bill.

The taxi came to a halt, Mum paid the driver and we walked towards the massive wooden door. Mum opened it and we walked through. You could see your face in the floor, it was so shiny, and I can remember treading very carefully in case I slipped. There were massive oil paintings on the walls. Oh, yes! Dr Frankenstein would have felt very much at home here!

We proceeded to the reception desk and were shown to the office of the governor of training. The governor seemed quite jovial. He shook Mum's hand, then mine, and indicated that we should sit down.

I was eventually shown to a side room and a kind lady brought me coffee and a piece of apple pie. Mum and the governor, meanwhile, were deep in conversation.

At last I was beckoned back into the governor's office. I knew that they had come to some agreement about my future – without any input from me, of course! They both looked extremely pleased with themselves and I had this niggling feeling that I was being forced into something against my will. I had this feeling of isolation once more – of being left out of decisions that would affect my future.

I was soon to realise, though, that Court Grange was a training establishment for people with all sorts of handicaps. The purpose was to maximise an individual's potential and to enable him or her to gain qualifications, obtain work and be self-sufficient.

I also knew that since I had lost my father Mum had had to work, and it dawned on me that she did not have the time or finances to look after me on a continuous basis.

I thought, 'Back to the drawing board, Hall! Get on with it and do your best!'

The time came for Mum to leave, and once again I had the feeling of desolation that being forsaken gives. I had understood, or had been led to understand, that we were just going to look around this time.

Of course, if I had thought at the time, I would have realised. One does not pack a case full of worldly possessions and take them somewhere if there is no intention to stay, does one?

Once again I felt deserted and lonely. The tears welled up and then flowed without control, cascading down my cheeks like miniature waterfalls, splashing on the polished floor. I was led to the governor's office and the consolation treatment began. In retrospect, though, I guess they were all very kind and only interested in what was best for me.

The governor commenced to outline what I would be doing at Court Grange. He introduced me to Mr White, who was to be my training officer. He was apparently a specialist in training the handicapped. This is an occupation that demands a great deal of patience and understanding, apart from a thorough knowledge of the various subjects.

Mr White introduced me to some of the staff, one of whom showed me round: where I was to sleep, where the toilets and bathroom were and, of course, where we had our meals and so on.

The dormitory was quite cosy and, as I far as I can remember, it was shared by eight young men. Of course it was empty at this stage because everyone was at work. I left my luggage by my bed and noted that I also had a locker and a chest of drawers – pretty much the same as at Rayners School.

We then proceeded to walk round the site and my guide, who was very knowledgeable, showed me round the various workshops, which included cooking, carpentry, decorating, engineering, bricklaying, plastering and gardening. Gardening included husbandry of animals – chickens, pigs, turkeys, cows and horses – and I was informed that, subject to my assessment, this was where I would be trained.

I hated gardening and looking after animals, and I told them so in no uncertain terms, but unfortunately I was informed that this was the only suitable training for a person with my particular disabilities. I learned later on that, in fact, it had already been decided. Mum had known what the plans were, and indeed she had to know to enable her to purchase all the correct and necessary workwear and equipment.

Once again I had been placed in a position and in a situation that I did not want to be in.

About a week passed and I was dreadfully unhappy. I asked to see the governor. He eventually sent for me and I explained that I did not like the farm or anything about it. He was very kind and sympathised with me, simultaneously trying to encourage me to stick with it and give it a few more weeks. I thought about what he said and decided to change my attitude after he explained that lengthy discussions had taken place between staff at Rayners School, my mother and the Court Grange tutors. They had decided that, perhaps, farm work and animal husbandry would suit me.

We would see! Oh, to be a farmer's boy!

The routine was as follows: the duty trainer used to wake us all at about 6 a.m. He would then return a few minutes later to make sure we were making a move. If we were not, then off came the bedclothes.

Needless to say, this could be embarrassing. We were all handicapped in some way, but I can assure you most of us were quite aware of the functions and wonders of our lower regions! Anyone looking in the bedroom could have mistaken it for a scout camp.

Eight erect tent poles greeted the morning sun, waiting for the canvas to cover their embarrassment. There was a lot of laughing and giggling, and it got the day off to a good start.

We got washed and shaved and ready for work, and

then we went off to the dining room for breakfast. The food was marvellous, and of course it was farm-fresh: fresh eggs, milk, vegetables, and dairy produce. I began to get a feeling of achievement. Everyone was eating something that I had helped to produce.

Before breakfast, though, I had to feed the chickens and collect the eggs – a lovely job in summer but a bit dicey, to say the least, in winter because I had to walk up a steep slope. Walking up wasn't too bad; but one icy morning, when I was on my way back down the hill with a basket full of eggs, I slipped and lost my balance.

My legs shot out horizontally and I landed in a grotesque heap, looking, for all the world, like an enormous uncooked omelette. Everyone, including the tutor, thought it was hilarious. The hens would have to work overtime!

As soon as breakfast was over, we returned to work, feeding the pigs, cleaning the stables, digging the garden, etc. All tools and equipment had to be thoroughly cleaned after use and stowed away in their proper places. I also had to learn how to use a diesel-driven plough, which was a massive bit of equipment controlled by a throttle and a clutch.

The controls were explained and the tutor demonstrated how to use it. I couldn't wait to have a go. The great moment came, but unfortunately I got a bit confused. My clutch became my throttle and vice versa. Anyway, whatever I did, the plough shot off at a rate of knots ploughing the first S-shaped furrow ever, and I was left pulling my face out of the mud with a lovely sucking sound. I was covered from head to toe, but I was determined to catch the monster and bring it under control. I staggered after the plough, which by now had made a pattern similar to a maze in the earth. At last I had hold of the handle and guided it back to the starting point.

The training officer was helpless with laughter. Thank God he had a sense of humour! He made a signal to stop the engine by drawing his hand across his throat, but I wasn't aware of this technical signal and it crossed my mind that he might want me to commit suicide. Eventually he caught up with me and switched the engine off, still helpless with laughter. I started to laugh as well, and it was some time before we regained our composure.

The days passed. One day was pretty much the same as another and we looked forward to the weekends. The establishment had access to a cottage on Dartmoor where, on some weekends, we were required to 'volunteer' for outward-bound training – i.e., hikes on the moors.

Looking after ourselves, cooking, washing and taking part in treasure hunts were all good character-building stuff.

I remember the first time I saw Dartmoor Prison. It was a damp, misty morning, and the thought of the hundreds of criminals locked away inside sent a shiver up my already cold, clammy spine.

Some weekends we were on duty – about every four weeks. The animals still had to be fed and cleaned out, eggs collected and the greenhouses tended. We grew tomatoes, cucumbers, marrows and all the usual garden vegetables; yes, we were fairly self-sufficient.

By this time I was beginning to make friends, and one day four of us decided to visit Newton Abbot. We were all about the same age (sixteen or seventeen), and we decided we were due for a change of image. First stop the barbers! I asked for a skinhead cut, and the remainder of my chums followed suit. I was becoming the leader of our group. They all seemed to follow me and do what I did. Next stop, a fashion store! We had been saving for months. The store catered specifically for skinheads. We pooled our money and bought all the gear we felt necessary to be proper skinheads: 'bovver boots' (brown), short-sleeved shirts and jeans rolled up at the bottom. I grew a moustache and we all tried to look mean, with our braces (Grandad-type) and long black coats with velvet collars. We looked the biz!

On our return to Court Grange, the governor did not recognise us at first, and when he did he was speechless for what seemed like ages. He stood with his mouth open, gawping and searching for something to say. He demanded an explanation. I am afraid I was rather rude. I told him to get lost. I stood up for myself and said I would wear what I wanted to wear in whatever fashion I chose.

The man was utterly gobsmacked. He did not quite know how to handle this rebellious character. Then he made it quite clear that whilst we were at Court Grange we would have to stick to the rules. We were also reminded that when we were out and about we represented the training establishment, and our behaviour was a reflection on the establishment. The governor made it quite clear that he did not like my new skinhead attitude.

Work became a bore and a chore, and we used to wish our lives away between weekends, impatient to get out of our overalls and into 'the gear'.

One particular weekend Torquay were playing Manchester United. Three of the lads from Court Grange and some skinhead chums from Newton Abbot were going to the match. The skinheads supported Torquay, so naturally I followed the gang. The match was a walkover for Manchester United. With players like George Best, Bobby Charlton and Dennis Law, Torquay didn't really stand a chance. Nevertheless we, the skinheads – the cult – and our cult skinhead girls, supported the underdogs and followed the rest of the skinheads at the inevitable end-of-match pitch invasion. It was like D-Day.

The football ground was a blur of flying fists, headbutts and 'bovver boots'.

I don't mind telling you, I was frightened. I had never experienced anything like this before. A Manchester United supporter ran towards me screaming, "Skinhead bastard!" and he struck me hard in the stomach. I doubled up, thinking I had been punched, but I soon realised that I had been stabbed. I was bleeding like a stuck pig and the knife was still sticking in me. I lost control. I pulled the knife out and all I could think of was revenge.

"You - - - - - - - bastard!" I yelled as I lunged towards my attacker.

I stabbed him in the guts, and my skinhead friends pulled me away. My clothes were now covered in blood, and we tied a cloth round my stomach to try to staunch the bleeding. I felt decidedly queasy. So this was being a skinhead – part of the cult, part of the gang.

My chums took me to Torquay Hospital – the pain was excruciating.

The doctor asked, "How the hell did this happen?"

One of my quick-thinking friends told him that I had

slipped and fallen on a broken bottle, gashing my side, but I am sure the doctor did not believe this – it was obviously a stab wound.

I have often wondered what became of the Manchester United fan I stabbed. I was quite horrified to realise what I was capable of when I lost control. At that moment I was not very proud of myself. The stitches were uncomfortable and kept pulling. I was not a happy chappie.

My three friends and I were dropped off at Court Grange. We managed to sneak in and keep the incident quiet. I guess we would probably have been expelled if the governor had found out. When a week or so had passed, I went back to Torquay Hospital and had the stitches removed. Ah, sheer bliss! They had begun to irritate.

This called for a few beers – with my skinhead friends, of course. I was now considered a bit of a hero, but underneath the jovial exterior, the jokes, the banter, the mickey-taking, I was more than a little concerned about the youth I had stabbed. I looked for reports in newspapers, both local and national, and I listened to news reports on the radio and television, but I read or heard nothing about the incident. I was filled with remorse and worry; it really concerned me that I was capable of such violence and could find myself in such a situation.

I was learning fast. The basic idea of the skinhead cult was fun and enjoyment, but fuelled by alcohol and drugs the fun very, very quickly and very often turned to violence, with all the blood and gore that goes with it.

I gradually withdrew from the skinhead cult. My hair started to grow, with the mandatory 'Beatles cut' at the front. I began to wear drainpipe trousers, a long jacket with a velvet collar, and black bumper-car shoes (I think the jacket was bright yellow). Boy, did I think I was the bee's knees! Of course I had, quite unintentionally, become a follower of another cult – the Teddy boys. I soon made lots of friends on the rock-and-roll scene. Life was a round of girls, booze and rockin' the night away. Although the Teds were not basically violent, once again booze and drugs infiltrated and the cool, calm image went out of the window.

One day we were sitting in a club in Newton Abbot, listening to a jukebox. Suddenly we heard the unmistakable sound of Lambretta scooters stopping outside the club.

'Here we go again!' I thought.

The mod boys and their birds entered the café like something out of a Wild West film, sprawled themselves all over the place and started taking the mickey out of my friends and me. I tried to calm things down. I did not fancy another visit to the hospital. Of course all my common sense fell on deaf ears – they were out for trouble.

Once again I found myself in the middle of a furious fight. Cursing and swearing, everyone was attacking everyone else with fists, feet, heads, chairs and tables. Bottles were smashing everywhere. The police arrived and they were soon getting heavily involved.

I noticed a back door – I think it was the fire exit.

I thought, 'That's for me.'

The door led to a back alley (fortunately the police hadn't cordoned it off) and I made my escape. When I stepped on to the lighted pavement I asked a passer-by what all the noise was in the club. Then I caught the bus back to Court Grange.

The more I became involved with violent situations, the less it affected me. At one time I was afraid and literally shook when threatened, but gradually I became immune to fear. I thought myself quite a tough guy. I was also under the impression that girls like tough guys, fighting and violence. This was probably true about some girls, but not the type of girl I was by now thinking about. I often thought at this time that it would be marvellous to have a stable relationship with someone of the opposite sex.

I also realised that involvement with cult groups like skinheads, Teddy boys, mods and rockers entailed drugs and violence to a degree and that a stable relationship or even a sensible lifestyle was impossible within such groups. It also frightened me that I was developing a casual attitude to violence and everything that went with it. I guess the college of life was teaching me the hard way.

I had to change.

CHAPTER III

THE NEW ERA

I was still at Court Grange. The recent events in my life had caused me to make a decision about my future. I knew now that if I was going to be successful in life, I had chosen the wrong route. Gradually I broke away from my skinhead and Teddy-boy friends. I decided once more, as teenagers do, to change my image and my life completely. I started to let my hair grow, stopped shaving and thought I'd smoke a pipe – that's a more manly thing to do.

One evening I decided to go to the cinema. I remember it clearly – Clint Eastwood in *The Good, the Bad and the Ugly*. I fancied an evening alone so I headed for Newton Abbot by myself.

Before settling into the front seats of the cinema, I decided to get my supplies in: popcorn, can of Coke, chocolate bars. I checked my baccy tin. Ah yes, plenty of baccy for my newly acquired manly-image pipe. (In those days, smoking was still permitted in many cinemas.)

I really enjoyed myself. Throughout the film I thought how utterly marvellous it would be to be like Clint Eastwood – so cool, calm and collected, with that steely gaze and the cigar in the corner of his mouth. Still, I thought, the pipe was just as cool. I demolished all the food I had bought, and I thought I would light up the jolly old pipe. This caused quite an uproar. The smoke I managed to generate would have done one of Her Majesty's destroyers proud, trying to hide our ships from enemy submarines. The problem was no one behind me or to the side of me for ten seats either side could see the film. Needless to say, the usherette was called.

She came charging down the aisle, torch flashing. She

31

spotlighted me in my seat, and requested that I move to the rear of the cinema, where, hopefully, I would not cause a nuisance.

"Sorry," I said. "No problem."

I proceeded to the rear of the cinema, standing on a few toes and stumbling into a couple of fat laps en route.

"Sorry. Oops! Sorry."

"Honestly!"

"Damned nuisance!"

"Should be chucked out!"

"Nutter!"

"Do you bloody mind!"

These were only a few of the friendly statements I received as I made my way to the rear of the cinema.

At last I reached the back row. Once again I settled down with my pipe, but it kept going out (much to the relief of everyone else).

This annoyed me and I suddenly thought, 'Clint smokes cigars – I'll nip out and buy five!'

Once again I was settled in the back row. I was sure the usherette fancied me – she kept staring at me. In retrospect I guess she was glaring, not staring, and she was probably wondering what she had done to deserve such a customer. I opened the packet of recently purchased King Edward slim cigars (just like Clint's). I reached for my lighter, placed the cigar in the corner of my mouth, raised the lighter and pressed my thumb.

Whoosh! A searing flame issued forth. I had forgotten it was adjusted for lighting my pipe. It seared into my beard, which caught fire. It was like a bloody forest fire. I screamed. Everyone's attention was now on the mad pipe-smoker from Court Grange. Meanwhile the usherette ran to the nearest fire extinguisher, came charging towards me, pointed it at my face and pressed the trigger. Sploosh! Right in my face! The jet was well aimed. The fire was extinguished.

The usherette said, "I'm so sorry, sir, but we couldn't have the cinema catching fire."

So there I was, with a singed beard, stinking of smoke and singed to the skin. The cinema was in an uproar. Clint Eastwood was forgotten; instead everyone was killing themselves laughing at this dishevelled, soaking-wet figure with long bedraggled hair, a singed beard and a soggy cigar hanging from between his lips. I decided to leave the premises. The last I remember was glancing back and seeing everyone laughing and the usherette standing with the spent extinguisher in her hand, her mouth open and eyes staring in disbelief.

At last I arrived back at Court Grange. I had never been so pleased to see the place in all my life. I decided to shave off what remained of my singed beard. A red scorch mark shaped like a star became visible under my chin, and as I continued to shave it became increasingly painful. For many years I had a bald patch on my chin to remind me of my introduction to Fire and Emergency Procedures as taught to British cinema usherettes. In retrospect, though, she may well have saved me from a horrendous disfigurement. If you ever read this, thank you, dear extinguishing usherette.

I still continued to smoke the pipe and occasional cigar, and, not wanting to carry an extinguisher about with me, I decided that a moustache was hair enough on any man's face.

It was now 1973 and I was nearing eighteen years of age. One morning I received a letter informing me that I had sufficient qualifications as a gardener and I would be leaving Court Grange soon to start work at the military hospital in Tidworth – not in the hospital, but in the grounds. Yes, they had even found a place of employment for me, and for this I was grateful. I was excited, a little apprehensive but full of hope for the next stage of my life and for the future.

I left Court Grange that December, just before Christmas. What a marvellous feeling it was to be a working man and coming home to Ludgershall to stay with my beloved mother for good. I felt a little sad when bidding everyone at Court Grange farewell, but those feelings were counterbalanced by the knowledge that I would be living at home, participating in family life and contributing to that life for the first time. Yes, life was taking on a new perspective.

I caught the train from Newton Abbot via Exeter to

Andover, then travelled by bus to Ludgershall. A far cry from the disabled little boy who had never heard a bird sing so many years before! My mother was obviously very proud and pleased with my progress. I was welcomed home with big hugs and kisses. I realised then how much I had missed this physical contact with my lovely mother and the warmth and affection she gave. I was indeed home at last and looking forward to my first real Christmas at home as a young man – the first Christmas when I did not have the thought in the back of my mind of having to leave home again afterwards.

CHAPTER IV

TIDWORTH GARRISON HOSPITAL

Prior to this Christmas, Mum had met and married an ex-army corporal. She was now known as Mrs Joe McGowan. I liked Joe, and I had attended their wedding as an usher. The wedding was in the summer of 1973.

Mum had all the information about my new job. I had to report to Tidworth Garrison Hospital on 4 January 1974; my wages would start at £40 per week and Mum had agreed to accept £10 a week for my keep.

Christmas 1973 was much the same as past Christmases, but now I was deep in thought with quite a bit of apprehension regarding my new job as a gardener at the military hospital. Thinking about my new job filled my head most of the holiday. I had always wanted to be involved with the military, but obviously as a civilian because my disability would not have enabled me to have any other role. So in a way I was achieving my ambition, albeit as a gardener with the MOD.

As explained, Christmas seemed to take a back seat, and I could not wait until 8 a.m. on 4 January. At last – the big day!

When I arrived at Tidworth Garrison Hospital, I hadn't a clue where to go. I remember walking towards a large door, not knowing quite which way to turn. I knocked – gently at first – but there was no response. I banged a bit louder!

"Come in, come in," boomed a military-type voice.

I opened the door very gingerly.

"Come in, laddie, come in. What can I do for you, my lad, eh what?"

I hadn't realised that this was the Colonel's office – that's right, the commanding officer's office.

I said, "I'm looking for the boss."

"I am the bloody boss, laddie," he replied. "What do ye want, eh?"

I tried to explain that I was the new gardener and I didn't know whom I was supposed to see or where I was supposed to go to meet my new boss.

The colonel was very kind.

He called, "Sergeant!"

A mountain of a man marched in – left, right, left, right, left, right. He stood to attention and saluted.

"Sir," he said.

"Take this young man to the head gardener's office and make sure he contacts Mr X the civilian property manager."

"Yes, sir," said the Sergeant. "Follow me, me lad," he said.

Left, right, left, right, left, right, he went. I found it difficult to keep up with him. At last we found the office. The Sergeant knocked on the door with his battering-ram fist.

"Come in," said a voice inside.

"One of yours," said the Sergeant and left – left, right, left, right, left, right.

"Good morning, John," the man behind the desk said. "You are now the head gardener of the Tidworth Hospital."

Notwithstanding I was the only gardener, I thought, 'Oh well, I'll be in charge of myself.'

The man showed me round my domain. Halfway round he remembered he had a meeting and asked RSM Fry to take over and escort me to my HQ (a large unkempt shed), which I shared with the hospital electrician. The tools of my trade were in the shed – most were rusty or out of date or both.

I spent the first few days complaining about the lack of proper equipment and tools. We had the best of everything at Court Grange, and, as stated previously, all tools and equipment were well maintained. Everything here was an absolute shambles! I also complained about the minute greenhouse, full of boxes of dead plants and old cracked plant pots.

The flower borders had been, and still were being, used as a short cut to the NAAFI and were as solid as concrete; the rose bushes had never been pruned and resembled enormous prickly oak trees; the weeds were in abundance, the main crop being *Dandelion ginormicus* – that is, bloody great dandelions, and every other species of weed you can think of. The place was a disaster, and of course it was my job as head gardener with no employees to put it right. A challenge is what I wanted, and a challenge is what I had got.

'Where the hell do I start?' I thought.

I started by disposing of all the dead plants in the greenhouse, and having a good clear-out. I then proceeded to check all of the tools, including the lawnmower. I made a list of my requirements. I dismantled the mower and sent the blades off to be sharpened.

I didn't take a great deal of notice or make any notes when I dismantled the mower. Consequently, when I came to reassemble it I was utterly baffled. It took about a fortnight or three weeks for me to fathom out the intricacies of rebuilding it. Meanwhile, the weeds continued their conquest of the garden.

Now to the weeds: I taped off the borders and put 'Keep Off' notices around the areas used as NAAFI footpaths, but I might as well have put a notice up in the Vatican telling the Pope not to pray! Squaddies continued to trample the borders like a herd of elephants. There was only one thing to do: get permission to lock the door leading to the pathways that should be flower borders. This I did. The borders were no longer invaded by stampeding hunger-crazed NAAFI-seeking squaddies.

One morning, I was loosening up some earth on the aforementioned borders when I was distracted by some very attractive nurses. I didn't realise, until I tried to walk away and tripped, that the garden fork had gone through my wellington boot, narrowly missing my foot, and pinned my foot to the ground.

Gradually, though, things took shape. Summer, with all of its extra duties, was looming ahead. I thought I had better get the mower ready for the onslaught. The mower was really old – an antique. It would not have looked out of place in the British Museum. In fact, Fred Flintstone probably had a similar model. I decided to attempt the main lawn outside the Colonel's office.

The big day came. I was quite excited at the prospect of cutting the grass outside the main building. I arrived early and topped up the mower with diesel. It spluttered, coughed, shook and belched smoke, but at last it started. I remembered the plough at Court Grange. The dew was still on the grass. As I took my first cut, a black velvety thing shot into the bucket. Examination revealed a beheaded mole. The poor little soul had probably popped his head above the grass, wondering what all the fuss and noise was, and wallop! – that's one way to stop the molehills, I suppose.

What I did not take into account was my walking disability. No matter how hard I tried, I could not walk in a straight line, so instead of nice Wimbledon-type mowed parallel lines, I had a series of criss-crossed uneven lines resembling a badly darned sock. The Colonel called for the RSM and said he had never ever seen anything like it in his entire life.

The RSM reckoned there was only one explanation – that I was drunk. There was no point at this stage in trying to explain the intricacies of my disability; I guess I would only have succeeded in getting deeper into the mire. The grass would grow within about a week to a fortnight. In the meantime I resolved to think of a way to overcome my balance problem so that I could mow a straight line.

Visitors were expected and the Colonel told the manager through the RSM that he wanted the weeds around the flagpole seen to before they arrived.

'Ah,' I thought, 'I'll get some weedkiller that kills weeds but does not harm roses, etc.'

I purchased the weedkiller and sprayed liberal amounts around the flagpole, which was in the middle of a bed of roses.

I remember thinking, 'I must turn the soil over.'

It was like concrete. Still, first things first: a generous dose of the old weedkiller.

As I was preparing to go home that evening it started to rain. I didn't think anything of it, but it rained and rained

38

all night and well into the following day. The pool around the concrete bed, in which the flagpole was the centrepiece, spilled on to and covered about three-quarters of the lawn. Imagine my horror – not to mention the Colonel's – when the sun evaporated the water on the lawn and revealed yellow grass. Yes, I had got rid of the weeds, but also the majority of the lawn.

"Call yerself a bloody gardener!" said the RSM. "The Colonel wants to see you, NOW!"

The Colonel was upset, to say the least.

"Have you never heard of just plain ordinary pulling bloody weeds out, man?" he said. "You realise that I could have you fired for this, don't you? Don't you! You have one month – one month – to put this bloody mess right or I'll have your guts for garters. Get out of my bloody sight!"

The next month proved to be the hardest month I can ever remember. I was determined to rectify the damage I had done. All I can remember was the hard, hard work. The lawn had to be returfed and fertilised. I remember having it confirmed that indeed it was fertiliser I was using and not weedkiller. My back ached, my hands were sore and blistered, and I felt like a prisoner of war. The nurses, who were all standing at the windows, had a great time laughing, but I thought, 'I'll show them! I'll show them!' The more they took the mickey, the more determined I became to rectify the mess I had made and to make some semblance of a garden.

As time passed, the mickey-taking nurses began to sympathise. When they were off duty they would come and talk to me, and they showed a great deal of kindness. I was physically attracted to one or two of them, and felt on occasion that I would like to date them and get to know them better, but I was so naive and did not know how to handle the situation.

One nurse introduced me to one of the surgeon officers, who apparently had been watching me and had admired my guts and determination. I christened him Dr Frankenstein. He thought this hilarious, and he said he thought my sense of humour was unique. We became quite friendly over the weeks that I was repairing the garden, and one day he noticed that I was not my usual perky self. He asked me what was troubling me.

I told him that for quite some time I had been bothered with a pain in my stomach, but it had suddenly got worse. It was quite unbearable. He asked me to go up to his surgery at lunchtime. My friend Frankenstein gave me a thorough examination and diagnosed a lump of fatty tissue pressing on a nerve.

He made a deal: "Move a willow tree in my garden for me," he said, "and I'll remove your fatty lump."

I explained that I had not had a great deal of experience with trees, but I promised to survey the situation. I said if I thought I was capable, I would move it for him. Frankenstein reckoned that he could remove my lump during the lunch hour with a local anaesthetic, thereby enabling me to continue work in the afternoon.

I was led to the garrison operating theatre.

"Get your top off and lie down," said Frankenstein.

I did what I was told. I don't mind telling you, I was more than a little nervous. Two injections around my lump made the area dead to the touch. I didn't feel a thing as he made an incision and squeezed the lump out. I remember thinking it looked a bit like Yorkshire pudding with gravy.

With no more ado, he stitched me up and told me it was OK for me to return to work. He gave me his home address in a village called Shipton Bellinger, and invited me to dinner. It was also an opportunity for me to survey the situation with regard to moving his tree from the rear to the front garden of his house.

I remember the meal vividly – especially when old Frankenstein was carving the meat.

"I bet this brings back memories, eh, John?" he said.

There was also some reference to vampires as he was pouring the rich red wine. Bloodthirsty lot, these surgeons!

The operation of moving the willow tree was more than I had bargained for, but I had eaten the man's meat and quaffed his wine so I decided to get on with it. First things first: after establishing where the tree was to be moved to, I dug a very large hole. I tried to guess the size of the roots and dug a hole to accommodate them. I then traced the roots of the willow tree and carefully and gently dug round them, trying to disturb them as little as possible. The roots were wrapped in a hessian sack and the lot then transferred to the prepared site. The hole I had prepared was fine, and I placed the roots, sack and all, in the hole. I very quickly shovelled in the soil, tamping it down as I went. A large wooden post for support and a belt round the tree and the post concluded the job, apart from watering it thoroughly and filling in the large hole now left in the back garden. To the best of my knowledge, the tree still stands today – a living memorial to my friendship with my personal lump-removing surgeon, Dr Frankenstein.

My work at the military hospital continued, and eventually the Colonel's lawn and borders were restored to their formal glory. It is hard to believe, but no sooner had I succeeded in the restoration than they decided to lay new pipelines around the flagpole area. This which meant, of course, undoing everything I had been working my guts out on for so long. The Colonel was raving but extremely sympathetic.

This was not the worst. That week we received the devastating news that the hospital was to close. I received a letter stating that I was no longer the head gardener; I was posted to another job. I was to report to the Sergeant Major at Tidworth Garrison to meet another colonel, who was to assign me to my new duties.

"Your new job", he said, "is picking up all the rubbish around the garrison, putting it in plastic bags and disposing of same – any papers, chip bags, or anything at all that is cluttering up the army garrison and married-quarters areas."

Can you imagine how I felt? Picking up other people's rubbish! I didn't know whether to laugh or cry. My department was an old garage full of plastic bags – the tools of my newly acquired trade. I felt so degraded. After all I had been through to try to improve myself, to end up like this! I just saw red. I was not going to accept this. Without further ado, I scribbled a note and handed it in to the office. I had resigned. I was now unemployed – a state I preferred to being a rubbish collector.

Mum came home to find me very upset. I told her what

had happened and that I had handed my notice in. I said I just could not take any more.

She said, "You fool! You fool!"

"I don't understand, Mum," I said.

She was very cross and, although she understood my motives, she then tried to explain about gratuities and pensions – all of which I had thrown out of the window instead of waiting until something else turned up or asking for a transfer.

My mother – God bless her – telephoned the Colonel and explained the situation. He said he would tear up my resignation and accept my apology, providing I turned up for work next day. I went to work next day and immediately requested a transfer to a better job.

About a month passed and a job became vacant at Larkhill. The work involved furnishing and replenishing married quarters. My only problem now was transport. I had to be out of bed at six o'clock to catch a bus to Amesbury. At Amesbury I had to catch another bus to take me to Larkhill in time for an eight o'clock start. Then, of course, there was the reverse problem at the end of the day.

Although I enjoyed the work and was getting on well, I asked for a transfer to Tidworth. To my surprise, I got it. So here I was at last, in a decent job, closer to home and, most importantly, happy.

CHAPTER V

THE CENTRAL VEHICLE DEPOT

I arrived at Tidworth. My job was to assist in replenishing married quarters, mending and assembling furniture and ensuring that each quarter had its quota of items prior to the families moving in.

There was a form. I think it was Form 1033 that we used as an inventory. The supervisor, Eddie, was very friendly and he took me under his wing. He was more like a father than a supervisor. Yes, he used to listen to all my problems.

I found the work interesting and varied. I was motivated and tried my best to do well, but once again there was a fly in the ointment. There always seemed to be at least one person who would not accept that because of my disability and deafness I always took a bit longer to do certain tasks.

I am afraid that Mr Hay, the boss, could not accept this. He openly discriminated against me and made me very uncomfortable indeed.

When one knows that one is not accepted, especially when working hard and doing one's best, it really is most exasperating. Once again I felt like asking for a transfer.

I thought I might try Ludgershall Central Vehicle Depot. I knew full well that Mr Hay was trying to provoke me. I did enjoy my work, but I felt that I had to make a move. I thought I would visit the vehicle depot and survey the situation. To this end, I arranged a couple of days' holiday and decided to pay them a visit.

The security guard was helpful, and subsequent to examining my MOD pass he directed me to Personnel, where I was given an appointment to speak to a personnel officer.

She asked what my problem was, and told me to take my time and explain why I wanted to move to Ludgershall. I explained the situation as best I could and also the fact that, because of my disability, Mr Hay had given me the impression that he wanted to get rid of me. I added that although the majority of my workmates were sympathetic, I could not really accept the situation and would rather move on.

She listened very closely to what I had to say and told me that there would be no guarantee that anything would change if I did move but she would try to help.

One day I arrived home, and to my surprise there was a brown envelope on the floor just inside the door, addressed to me. I was to report to Mr Jim Smith in the traffic section at Ludgershall Central Vehicle Depot.

I couldn't wait to tell Hay that I was leaving.

He said, "You can't do that. You're sacked!"

He phoned head office in Bulford and found out that indeed I did have a legitimate transfer and he could not sack me. Yes, I was learning fast how to go about things!

Once again I was moving to a fresh start even closer to home – in fact, within cycling distance. The day I left Tidworth, I received a nice card signed by all of my mates and a case to keep music cassettes in. The lads knew I loved music.

It was now 1976. I had to report to Jim Smith, in charge of traffic, and I soon learned that part of my job was to assist in loading vehicles, securing them on the carriages and ensuring that they were correctly labelled. I then had to place a large tarpaulin over each vehicle to keep out the elements and generally get them ready for transportation by rail.

We had some fun with the tarpaulins, especially on windy days. On one such day I ended up on the siding, freezing cold, in a howling gale with a bloody great tarpaulin covering me. The damned things were such a weight that once you got trapped underneath you couldn't move.

The work was very demanding physically. The 'normal' employees found it hard enough, so you can guess how it affected me. I was determined, though, to make a go of it,

44

and I persevered to overcome my difficulties.

They were a good crowd of lads, and at that time skiffle music was all the rage. We decided to have a skiffle group.

Good old Trevor was on teachest bass; a locker and table served as drums; and yours truly was the vocalist. I had never realised just how bad my voice was! They taped this horrible din, and when they played it back the tears just rolled down everyone's faces. There was uncontrolled laughter. I can never remember laughing so much. My sides literally ached and ached. We couldn't do anything for laughing.

Now, of course, everyone realised that I had a terrific sense of humour. It seemed to break the ice and I became more and more accepted. The more I became accepted, the harder I worked to get on.

Yes, I was thinking about promotion.

CHAPTER VI

PROMOTION

There was a noticeboard in our department upon which various pieces of information were pinned, including weekly and daily orders. One day a notice stated that a storekeeper was required as an assistant to the senior storekeeper. This would mean promotion and a larger salary. I found out through various means what the job consisted of, and I thought I might be able to cope. The job mainly entailed checking military vehicles for damage against a checklist and assisting the senior storekeeper by feeding in document information.

I had one big drawback: my reading and spelling left a lot to be desired because of my handicap. I had to seek help to fill out the application form. I also realised that I would have difficulty hearing on the telephone. Nevertheless I forged ahead and, with the help of my workmates, I managed to fill in the form with my own handwriting, such as it was, and sent in my application.

I must say that none of my friends held out much hope of my being successful, but I was determined not to be a labourer all my life.

About one week later I received a letter asking me to attend a promotion board.

The big day arrived and, needless to say, I was very nervous indeed, as I had not received much encouragement from my workmates.

"Mr John Hall."

My name was called out and I entered a room.

"Sit down, Mr Hall," said a chap who I assumed was in charge of the proceedings.

I knew two people on the board so I began to feel a little more at ease.

They asked me all sorts of questions: "Will you be able to cope?" "Will you be able to fill out the various forms and actually check vehicles?" "What about hearing the telephone and the fire bell?" and so on.

I answered all of their questions honestly. I told them that I did not know if I could cope, but I was willing to work hard and overcome any difficulties that may crop up. I also assured them that I learn quickly and that I felt that I was capable of doing the job.

Some of the board members seemed to know my situation very well. I think they had done their homework prior to the interview.

Approximately two weeks passed. I arrived home and there was another brown official-looking envelope on the floor inside the door. I tore it open and read, convinced that it was bad news.

The letter read, 'It gives me great pleasure to inform you that . . .'

Yes, I had been accepted. I had the job. I was now assistant to the senior storekeeper. I had a title. I was no longer a labourer. I was having the last laugh.

Quite a few of my colleagues were now very upset indeed.

My first day with Trevor was very helpful. If ever you read this, Trevor, I want you to know that I could never have managed without your perseverance and patience in explaining all the aspects of what was expected of me. In retrospect, I feel that you may have had something to do with my getting the job.

The tasks included identification of vehicle damage, noting any damage in the correct forms and documenting the information. I had to learn the correct methods of access and egress to and from vehicles, and I had to be familiar with all the regulations concerning health and safety at work.

As time passed by, I got into the swing of things and I believe I was doing a satisfactory job of work. I purchased

47

a dictionary and found it invaluable to check the correct words and the correct spellings for all the documents for which I was responsible.

The senior storekeeper, Mr Vockins, retired and Jim Smith moved to D-Med, which was concerned with sending medical supplies all over the world. The new senior was a lady named Marion, and my immediate supervisor was Anton. We all got on very well, and as time went by we developed a very good relationship.

When, on occasion, there was little work to do, we had a good time playing cards and darts – and of course there was our skiffle group, including me tearing the vocals apart.

Yes, life was very good; I was accepted in my place of work. One of the most important things in life is to be accepted by your peers and to be happy at work.

One day there was a document required from a Centurian tank. This day was wet and miserable. I opened the hatch and leaned into the turret, holding the hatch open. The turret was wet; my hand slipped, and down came the hatch on my head.

I thought I was probably severely injured, and I couldn't move for a minute. I managed to open the hatch, and although my head throbbed I could not feel any blood. I stayed a couple of minutes on top of the tank until I recovered. I dismounted and went to our locker room. I confirmed that there was no blood, but my head and neck were badly bruised.

The incident was reported, but nothing further transpired. My mother's advice still rings in my ears: "Be more bloody careful!" I became more aware of the dangers around me and the necessity to be more careful when working on or near the vehicles. Before I attempted anything, I had to think of my disability, balance, position and so on. Since that day I can put my hand on my heart and say I have never been involved in a similar incident.

I was now a fully established storekeeper. I was quite happy to work away for a year or so, but I still thought of advancing myself. About 1978 I decided it was time to move on and gain more experience.

A system existed whereby if one found someone in

another department who agreed to swap, and it was also agreed by the officer in charge, then a swap of departments with the subsequent gain in experience was possible. I tried and was successful in acquiring a swap to the kit stores. This I thought might lead to promotion to a senior storekeeper.

Once again I was in a new department, learning new procedures, with different forms and mountains of paperwork. The boss, Mr Gate, put me to work with Peter Smart the senior storekeeper and Jackie. Dear Jackie! She was very patient and showed me the ropes. Everyone was helpful and kind, and for this I thank them.

Of course, at this time there were no computers and details of every item had to be entered in a ledger. All items of equipment were kept in bins, all labelled – for example, 'ROW A, BIN 22, Drivers, screw for the use of'. Each vehicle had items of equipment particular to that vehicle, such as tools, spares, guns and ammunition.

I had been in the kit stores about six months before everything started to fall into place. The kit stores to this day are using the same racking system, data boards and coding. I am sure it could all be simplified.

My suggestions about using a computer and microfiche were ridiculed. They just did not want to know, or possibly they did not have the patience to listen to my ideas.

They probably thought, 'Oh, it's just poor old handicapped John. What does he know?'

Anyway, can anyone know the frustration that a person in my position feels when all suggestions are simply sidestepped with a pat on the shoulder and a wink. People don't even realise that the deaf can see the winks and the nudge-nudges and the nods that so-called 'normal' people communicate with in the presence of the handicapped. Well, it bloody well hurts, you know. It hurts!

I know I had some well-thought-out practical ideas, but, as explained before, they were all brushed aside. What the hell were they afraid of? Surely they could have had the good manners to listen. I guess they must have thought that because of my speech impediments I was also stupid.

All I wanted was to be heard. If my ideas were rubbish, then fine. Point out to me where they are wrong, but don't, for God's sake, pat me on the back and wink at one another as though I don't understand what you are thinking. There are numerous persons who could be named who knowingly or unknowingly jeopardised my career. There was a great deal of laughing and joking at my expense. I think there is something very evil and sinister about people who laugh and joke at the expense of the afflicted. I have known many who are more afflicted than I am, but I have always tried to help them. I never joked or laughed at the deformities or inadequacies of others.

Many, many evenings I rushed home and went straight upstairs to lie on my bed, sobbing, sobbing my heart out through sheer unadulterated frustration. But through all of this came a determination to prove that John Hall was no ordinary disabled person. I resolved to fight and fight to prove that there was more to me than met the eye.

I attempted four times to be promoted to senior storekeeper. Each time I was required to write a letter by hand explaining my wish; then all candidates were called to attend a promotion board.

The board consisted of five or six senior civil servants sitting at a crescent-shaped table. They asked what I thought about various current affairs and also fired questions at me regarding the duties of a senior storekeeper. I was convinced then, and I am convinced now, that because of my disabilities the board had already made up its mind that I was not the person for the job.

This was confirmed for me when at my fourth attempt they started discussing my disabilities – a subject that I thought had been exhausted at my first, second and third promotion boards. I became so angry and felt so humiliated that, after a tirade, I stomped out in a rage. In retrospect, this of course did my case no good whatsoever.

The main objections I feel were my inability to hear the telephone clearly and possibly my writing, but, as I explained, there are such things as amplifiers and I was willing to work really hard to improve my writing. Of course they were looking for people who already were qualified, not for people who were still learning, or improving.

Each board asked the same boring questions, mainly

with regard to my disabilities. I did not want to discuss what disabilities I have, but what I was capable of doing. All I asked was for a chance to prove that I was capable of holding the job down. I even suggested that they promote me on a trial basis: if I was found to be unsuitable after, say, two or three months, they could demote me to my original status. I will never understand why the MOD do not do more to assist the disabled. We also have hopes and aspirations! I am convinced that they already knew who they were going to promote before the board even sat. In my estimation, it really was a great waste of time.

Everyone's records are perused, and points are noted, long before the promotion board sits. Consequently board members enter the meetings with preconceived ideas about a candidate's capabilities. Can you imagine what people who did not really know me must have thought when they read my records?

'Deafness and spasticity affecting co-ordination of the legs. Also finds difficulty writing accurately and quickly.'

Ah well, they also reckoned I did not have the necessary education or word power – whatever that is! Of course I never did think that my disability had anything to do with their decision not to promote me. I felt within myself that I could do the job, that there are ways to compensate for my disabilities.

The last promotion board I attended once again commenced to discuss my disabilities in detail. I just could not take it any more. I stood up, looked at them all in disgust and walked out.

Needless to say, I have never tried again. I now know I was never ever going to be passed by this board or any other. I had been pigeonholed. I lacked paper qualifications and certificates, but I knew my job backwards and all I desired was an opportunity to prove that I was capable of being a supervisor.

I did go to college to attempt to acquire the necessary certificates, but I failed. Needless to say, I was devastated. My world crumbled. I felt useless – an absolute failure. I knew that I was doomed to be a storekeeper for the rest of my life.

I had tried four times, but each time the board

concentrated on trying to convince me that my disabilities would prevent me from doing the job that I knew I could do. It was all such a waste of time and effort. My spirits sank lower and lower and I sought solace in the bottle. I felt utterly rejected. Of course the more I drank and felt sorry for myself, the more miserable I became; the more miserable I became, the more I drank and felt sorry for myself. My drinking and misery began to have an effect on those around me. I was making life hell for my family – my mother in particular. I became a self-centred, self-pitying and all-round miserable bastard.

Mind you, no one knew at the time the mental torture that rejection had embedded in my mind. I felt so worthless, and I was generally depressed.

CHAPTER VII

THE LUDGERSHALL HALF-MARATHON

One evening in 1983 I was drinking at Ludgershall Sports Club. Some people were congregated round the noticeboard.

One said, "Hey, John, this is just up your street – the Ludgershall Half-Marathon in aid of charity."

I walked over and looked at the notice.

"No way!" I said. "I can hardly walk let alone bloody run."

"Oh, you - - - - - - - - coward! You - - - - - - - useless spastic coward!" one said.

I went home and switched on the television. The words kept ringing in my head: '- - - - - - - coward! You - - - - - - - useless spastic coward!"

'I'll show them,' I thought.

So back down to the sports club I went and put my name on the list of runners amidst comments of "You'll never make it, stupid prat!" "You'll be done in after 100 yards, you - - - - - -!" and "Don't do it, John; it'll kill you." (That was one of the more considerate remarks.)

Meanwhile I was thinking, 'God, what have I done? I am going to make an absolute fool of myself.'

I was dreadfully overweight (about 18 stone) and very unfit into the bargain. I had been doing nothing but bingeing on food and drink for months, and here I was enlisting for a half-marathon for charity. Charity, for Christ's sake! It was me who needed charity.

One night I got so drunk that I thought I would go for a dip in the river running under the D-Med railway bridge – somewhere in the drunken recesses of my brain I thought it was a river. I leaped over the bridge and fortunately landed on the embankment, sustaining minor abrasions and bruising. God, what a state I was in! If I had landed on the steel track, I guess that would have been the end.

Another thing I hadn't bargained for was that, through sheer ignorance, I did not realise that a half-marathon is about thirteen miles. What had I let myself in for? I dared not, and could not, back out.

Needless to say, my mother tried to talk me out of it.

"For God's sake," she said, "fit people find it hard-going. You are nearly 18 stone, unfit and disabled. If you want to kill yourself, go ahead; just don't blame me if you end up in hospital. But, John, be sensible! It's thirteen miles, for Christ's sake! That is a very, very long way. You could end up very, very hurt indeed. The decision is yours."

She knew it was useless to try to persuade me to back out. She, of all people, knew how determined and stubborn I could be.

Everyone obviously thought I was stark staring bonkers, so I had to prepare more or less by myself.

'Now then,' I thought, 'what do proper athletes do?'

Of course, I had to get a tracksuit, some training shoes, T-shirts, etc. I had watched my hero Sebastian Coe many times on TV. I had to do some training before the big day.

I donned my tracksuit, put on my trainers and started to jog. I had gone less than half a mile when it began to dawn on me how stupid I was being. I suffered from severe stitch, my groin ached, thick phlegm developed in my chest, and I coughed and spluttered. I felt decidedly ill. The twenty or so cigarettes I smoked a day obviously didn't help (what a bloody state I was in!), and here I was volunteering for a half-marathon to help the disabled. Ah well, they say charity begins at home.

The exact date eludes me. All I know is that it was summer. I felt a mixture of elation, excitement, apprehension, fear and determination. I kept thinking, 'I'll show them! I'll show them! Even if I've got to crawl on all fours, I'll show the bastards! I can do it – I can do this thing.'

Mum said, "I can't come, John; I've got too much housework to do."

I know now, of course, that she was afraid I would make a prat of myself in front of everyone.

She gave me a cuddle and said, "Be careful. Good luck, son. Be careful."

"I'll be OK," I said. "Don't worry."

I knew I was not prepared, but I had committed myself and something deep within was driving me on. I thought of Sebastian Coe. Would he give up? No way, and neither would I. I just had to prove to myself and to everyone else that I had the guts to do this.

Sebastian would warm up, so I decided to have a little jog to the starting point – the sports centre. That was an utter waste of time because we waited about half an hour before the off. Some people started to take an interest when they realised I was determined to start. They gave me tips, like rubbing my leg muscles with wintergreen, not letting myself get too cold, etc.

At last we were issued with numbers. I can't remember mine. I was in a bit of a trance – a dreamlike state. I could not believe I had let myself in for this.

"You'd better go to the loo," I was advised, "because it's not really on to do it on the way round."

I took the advice – and thank God I did! Without going into detail, I thoroughly cleared all systems, took my tracksuit off, pinned on my number and placed all my gear in my bag. We were told to prepare to start. The starting point was on Somme Road. More than 100 people were taking part and I was the only person with any disability. No one even knew I was there. By this time everyone was concentrating on their own race. I was very, very frightened. I did not realise what lay ahead.

We lined up.

"Two minutes to go," said the starter. He stood on a platform with his starting pistol. "All set."

Bang! The pistol fired and we were off.

I just had to charge ahead. This of course showed my inexperience. Before I had charged 100 yards I felt absolutely knackered. I coughed, wheezed and spluttered while everyone passed by; can you imagine how I felt when everyone disappeared over the horizon? My legs felt like jelly. I bent double, trying to induce some oxygen into my lungs. I thought, 'What a prat! What a bloody prat!'

Mum was right as usual: there was more to this than a new tracksuit and trainers. I stood there alone, and I felt so angry with myself. Once again I was letting myself down.

I kept thinking, 'Sebastian Coe wouldn't stop. Sebastian Coe would keep going. If he can - - - - - - - do it, so can I. So can I.'

Then I realised I had another thirteen miles to go.

Eventually the feeling returned to my legs and they stopped shaking. I stamped my feet to encourage the circulation and off I went again. I did realise that there was a long, long way to go. There were posts at various intervals telling us how far to go, how far to refreshment areas, etc. I was dying of thirst, and a post informed me there were two and a half miles to the first drinking area. The route ran towards Perham Down, then turned right up a gradient towards Station Road, Tidworth, turned left at the traffic lights then on towards Shipton Bellinger.

My feet felt like red-hot lead weights; my socks by this time were soaked with sweat. My feet began to chafe. I felt generally uncomfortable. I began to realise that I was developing large blisters on the pads of both feet. God, I wished I had listened to my mother! Because I was so fat, my shorts began to cut into my groin. Now I was breathless, dying of thirst, had sore, blistered feet and a red-raw groin. Isn't life a gas!

An official pointed out the direction I had to take towards Kimpton. I was informed that I was a good mile behind the next competitor, and this was a woman.

At last, a drinking post! It was only orange juice, but I can never ever remember a drink tasting so good. It was sheer and utter bliss.

Off I went again. I tried not to think of my aching legs, the blisters and, by now, the blood running down my thighs from my too tight shorts. Occasionally I staggered and just walked, swaying from side to side; then I would break into a little trot, then a stagger. I must have been a pitiful sight.

A man came alongside in a car and said, "Come on, mate. You look all in. I've got to collect the stragglers."

I said, "Go away. I'm going to finish this if it - - - - - - -
kills me. Go away and leave me alone."

At this point I thought, 'What a prat I am!'

I had gone through Kimpton and was now approaching
Ludgershall. If only I could keep going!

'I must keep going. I'll show the bastards! I'll show them!'

What a state I was in! Blistered feet, blood running down
my legs – my body ached everywhere. God, I felt rough!

I thought, 'If I just make the railway bridge, I'll be OK.'

I reached the bridge. People were cheering me on –
cheering me, John "Useless Spastic Bastard" Hall. Cheering
me! I kept running with renewed strength. There was a
police motorbike in front with lights flashing and an
ambulance behind me.

As I ran through Ludgershall village quite a few villagers
lined the route. All were cheering me on.

"Good old John! Go on, John – you can do it. You can
do it."

'Christ, they've changed their tune,' I thought.

Unbeknown to me the route went directly over the
railway bridge to home, but I turned right towards D-Med.
The road was deserted except for one kind person who
gave me an ice cream. Many, many thanks, whoever you
are. God bless you.

By this time every movement was automatic. I had gone
through the pain barrier and all I wanted to do was reach
the finishing post. I plodded on and on back to the main
road, and the last stage uphill to Castledown School and
the finish.

I turned right into Castledown. To my surprise there
were hundreds of people there cheering – cheering me
home and blowing horns.

"Go on, John! Go on, John!" they called.

Anyone would have thought I was first instead of
second last!

"You're nearly there. You can do it. You can do it."

I felt wonderful – the blisters and pain were forgotten.

I saw the finish tape, and imagine my utter elation and
joy when I saw my mother standing there with her arms
outstretched. I fell into her arms. She hugged me, squeezed
me and kissed me.

"Well done, son! Well done!" she said through her tears
– she was crying. "You've proved us all wrong. You've
proved us all wrong."

I was escorted to the first-aid room immediately. I was
ashen-white and felt quite sick. I went into the ladies' loo
by mistake. Anyway, who cares? I'd just run thirteen
bloody miles!

Spasticity, deafness, blistered bloody feet, a bleeding
groin, aching tired legs – I had the lot and I did it, I did it.

By the way, I wasn't last. The woman in front of me
took the wrong turning and ended up somewhere in
Andover, so I was not last!

The events that followed are a blur. I was so weak that I
cannot really remember much about what happened
immediately after the run. All I wanted to do was get home
and get straight into a hot bath. This I did. I fell asleep in
the bath and when I woke up the water was barely tepid.

I attempted to get out of the bath, but my muscles had
seized up; I could hardly move. Eventually I struggled to
my feet, very gingerly putting my weight on them. I lifted
one after the other and examined my soles. They were
absolutely red-raw, and it was agony just trying to dry
them. I struggled out of the bath and had to walk on the
edge of my feet to try to keep the soles from touching the
carpet. Climbing the stairs seemed like attempting Everest.
God, I was in a frantic state!

Suddenly there was a knock on the door. I struggled to
my feet and made for the door. I must have looked like
some demented Highland dancer – arms up in the air to
try to maintain my balance and each foot coming into
contact with the floor for less than a microsecond. Put to
music, I doubt if Lionel Blair could have followed me that
day.

I opened the door. It was a lady reporter from the
Andover Advertiser and a photographer. They had come
to interview me. This confused me. Why on earth were
they bothering to interview me? I was last – er, second
last – in the bloody race. Surely they should be interviewing
the winner, not me. I had only completed the run to prove
to myself and to those plonkers in the sports club that

handicapped or disabled, or whatever you like to call it, I was capable of completing the course. I guess someone had contacted the newspaper and classified me as some sort of local hero.

The reporters were fascinated by the fact that someone with my disabilities had even attempted the run. I guess they wanted a story. They asked the usual questions: Why had I done it? etc.

I told them I just had to take myself to the limit to see how far a person with my particular disabilities could actually go. I said I didn't think I had reached my limit – in fact, I told them my sights were set on the London Marathon.

The report read as follows:

John's Back in Training

John Hall, the handicapped Ludgershall runner, is in training again for a half marathon in Reading on March 25th. He said "I will be on the start line for the Round Table Fun Run at Thruxton Circuit." John, who lives with his mother in Old Common Way, earned the congratulations of a large crowd when he forced himself to complete a road race around the village of Ludgershall in aid of The Fireman's Fund. He also competed in the annual Boxing Day Run at Collingbourne Ducis and now runs for The British Sports Association for the Disabled. He has already collected £150 for charity.

I was very impressed by the report; everyone in the village was treating me like a hero. Needless to say, I enjoyed this. I felt elated and, for the first time, as though I had been totally accepted. Having mentioned the London Marathon, I became a little apprehensive regarding how to go about it. I guessed that a good place to start would be the local sports centre.

They advised me to join a local athletic club, and they named the Collingbourne Harriers as a possibility. It was felt that they were best equipped to advise me about correct training preparation and eventual entry into the bigger marathons, including the London Marathon and – who knows? – perhaps even the New York Marathon.

I applied and was accepted as a member of the Collingbourne Harriers; they had read of me in the paper and took me under their wing. My training commenced: short runs twice a week to start with, gradually increasing in distance. I was also advised to stop smoking. This I did. My diet was also important. I cut out a lot of fats and reduced my drinking of alcohol to a bare minimum. Gradually I lost weight. Before long I tipped the scales at about 12 stone (about 76 kilos) – not bad from 18 stone (114 kilos). My breathing improved and running became less and less difficult. I began to enjoy it. The more I enjoyed it, the further I ran; the further I ran, the fitter I got. I felt wonderful. I was determined to drive myself to the limit, be a disabled guinea pig and just see what my limitations were.

My heart and lungs, which are very strong, were now dictating I run faster and faster. Sometimes they dictated too fast and I just toppled over, forgetting that my legs did not always do what I intended. Perhaps I had reached my personal peak.

I was now preparing for the London Marathon, but prior to that there was a half-marathon at Reading.

CHAPTER VIII

THE 1984 READING HALF-MARATHON

One of my new friends, a nice guy named Len, who was in the athletic team, gave me a lift in his car. As we headed towards Reading the weather was favourable and I hoped it would stay that way. I recalled my first competitive race and the mistakes I had made – absolutely no preparation whatsoever and starting off like a greyhound. That was why I had ended up knackered after 100 yards. The pain, the misery, the skin rubbing off my feet, the blood running between my chafed legs: I remembered all this as we approached Reading. But this time I was better prepared; I had been training with experts. I was fitter than I had ever been in my life, and I had listened to the advice offered by my colleagues.

We arrived at Reading in plenty of time to get changed and be issued with our numbers. My number for this half-marathon was 3287. The plan of the route looked complicated, but it was explained during the preliminaries that there would be plenty of guides and also markers and posters to assuage my growing doubts and fears. My clothes were placed in a labelled plastic bag and stowed in a bus provided for the purpose.

I started to stretch and warm up, as advised during my training sessions to help prevent cramp. My stomach was churning, but I felt strangely confident. I was thinking through my strategy. This time I would not go like a bullet from a gun and get cramps and feel sick after a few yards.

No, this time I paced myself with the other runners for the first few miles – I just jogged along.

Six or seven miles into the half-marathon I started to push myself. I was breathing well, my lungs felt easy and

61

my heart felt strong. I felt really comfortable.

The crowds lining the route were very supportive, cheering us on. I felt wonderful, marvellous. What a difference from my first attempt! I didn't feel at all tired and did not find it necessary to stop at every drinks point, though to prevent dehydration I had to stop at a few.

I just could not believe how fit and well I felt, but I contained myself, stifling the urge to push myself too hard. I had learned my lesson with regard to that. I was now becoming an experienced runner, and I was running well within my capabilities. This was a great boost to my morale – a far cry from the self-pitying drunken bum I had been becoming. Now I felt I was somebody worthwhile. I was doing my own thing and proving to everyone that, even if I am handicapped, it would never stop me from trying.

I kept plodding on – flip, flap, flip, flap. The sound of my feet hitting the road maintained a regular rhythm. I saw the finishing line. Good God, I could not believe I had completed more than thirteen miles and still felt so fresh. I crossed the line.

Other members of the Collingbourne Harriers were amazed that I had finished so comfortably and in such a good time. I was placed somewhere in the middle.

All that was running through my mind now was the Big One the following year – the London Marathon in 1985.

All competitors who completed the Reading Half-Marathon were presented with a medal. This was my second medal now. I will never forget the pride I felt when this beautiful young lady placed the medal ribbon over my head. I kissed the medal and thought, 'This is for you, Mum. This is to prove to you and to the world that I, John Hall, can achieve things despite my disabilities.'

I knew she would be so proud of me, I was just sorry she had not been there. Little did I know it, but at the time my mother was quite ill. No one would have known by looking at her; she was still my beautiful, gorgeous mother.

CHAPTER IX

LOSS

Members of the Collingbourne Harriers assisted me to complete the necessary forms and pay my entry fee for the London Marathon. They explained that applicants were not always successful, but – lo and behold! – I was. I was now committed to running twice as far as I had ever run before – 26 miles 388 yards. Now to get down to some serious training.

I still felt elated after my success in the Reading Half-Marathon, but my mind was now filled with thoughts of the gruelling 26.2 miles. I thought, 'Could I possibly have turned back at Reading and run all the way back to the starting point?' This was a daunting thought, but I was determined to be positive. I kept thinking, 'I can do it, I can do it.' I had to prove I could do it.

About this time Mum arranged for me to go and visit my sister Gail in Yorkshire. She said she required the room as she had some friends coming to stay from Bournemouth. I thought this all a bit strange. I still was not aware of the extent of her illness.

I was sitting in my sister's by the fire reading a newspaper – in fact, waiting for dinner – when there was a heavy knock on the door. My sister opened the door. It was the police. She thought I was in trouble, but they explained that a member of the family had to telephone Winchester Hospital. My sister did this. It was confirmed that my mother had had a nasty fall, but they would not explain any more at this stage. It was advised that I go down immediately. Gail was very upset.

Dave, Gail's husband, drove me to Harrogate, where I caught a train to Leeds and eventually Winchester. I cannot remember much about the journey. All I could think of was my beautiful, warm, lovely mother, who was lying injured and unwell in Winchester Hospital. I did not, even then, realise how seriously ill she was.

The journey seemed to take for ever – but then journeys always do when you are desperate to get somewhere or to be near someone.

Eventually I arrived in Winchester. I remember walking up a steep hill with two heavy suitcases towards the hospital.

When I arrived, the Nurse was very kind. She offered me tea and biscuits. I accepted gratefully. I suddenly realised I hadn't eaten for hours. I asked how my mother was; the Nurse replied that she would telephone the Doctor. She did and advised I should wait until the Doctor spoke to me personally. The Doctor arrived and immediately began to explain that my mother had had a very serious fall at home. She had fallen backwards down the stairs, severely gashing her head and badly bruising the rest of her body. The Doctor explained that my mother was now in a coma, and he asked me to do what I could to try to make her regain consciousness.

He left me alone with my mother. She looked as though she was fast asleep. I was very upset. I held her hand tenderly.

I spoke to her: "Mum, Mum, this is John – your son. I love you. Please, please wake up. What happened? Why did you fall? Wake up, Mum. Please wake up. I'm here with you."

It might have been ten minutes or maybe as much as thirty minutes, I don't know, but suddenly she spoke. I was startled. She said, "Is that you, John?"

I replied, "Yes, Mum, it's me."

"Where's Gail?" she asked. "I want Gail. I want to see Gail."

"Gail is at home. I will look after you," I said. "You've had a very nasty accident. What happened to you?"

She could not remember anything that happened; she didn't realise that she had split her head open and that the stair carpet and walls had been drenched in her blood.

"Rest now. Rest, Mum," I said, stroking her hand gently.

I'll see if I can stay here, and I'll see you in the morning."

I could not get the blackness of her eyes out of my mind. When she opened her eyes it was like looking into black, empty sockets. This was caused by internal bleeding and bruising, I was informed later.

I was allowed to stay in the hospital. I cannot ever remember being so cold and depressed. I could not sleep; I was wracked with concern and worry. My poor, poor mother! What she must have been going through! I did love her so much.

There was worse to come.

Next morning I awoke, had breakfast and went in to see my mother. I was amazed. She was sitting up and she seemed quite bright. The doctor said they were going to send her to Southampton for neurological tests. I gave her a kiss, told her I would be back as soon as possible, and left.

Apparently the reason she had sent me to Yorkshire was so that she could accommodate some friends from Bournemouth. There was no evidence of their presence when I arrived home; instead I was greeted by Tom and Barbara Humphries, who, I was informed later, had cleaned up all the bloodstains and mess on the stairs so that I would not be upset when I returned. God bless you, Tom and Barbara! You always have been, and always will be, two of my best friends. You are always there with advice and humour; always there when I need someone. Thank you from the bottom of my heart. I could not have survived the next few months without you.

It began to dawn on me that I didn't have a clue about housekeeping, about bills, about balancing the budget – about anything. My mother had taken care of everything. I was utterly and completely lost.

Mum's bank froze her account. I couldn't get her signature, so bills began to go unpaid and mount up. More bills kept coming through the letter box, and, of course, this worried me more. What with all this financial worry and Mum lying in hospital, I sometimes didn't know which way to turn. I didn't sleep for nights on end and I began to look like a zombie.

It was suggested that I make an appointment to see the

bank manager to discuss Mum's account and perhaps arrange an overdraft. This I did.

After the neurological tests, Mum was sent back to hospital in Winchester. The next time I visited, the Sister informed me that the Doctor wished to see me. As soon as I saw him, I could sense that he had bad news. The look on his face said it all.

"There is no easy way of putting this, John," he said. "Your mother has a tumour on her brain the size of an egg, and she also has cancer of the breast. She has, at the outside, perhaps two years to live."

Four weeks later she had deteriorated even more and her life expectancy was reduced to six months.

Oh, my God! What a shock! What a feeling of utter helplessness! This is where the 'if onlys' come in: if only I had cared more, if only I had been a better boy, if only I had tried to help her more, if only I had loved her more, if only, if only, if only. Oh, Mum, my darling, beautiful Mum, I loved you so much. But I had to try to be strong for her sake. I had to be strong.

The people at work were very supportive at this stage. Any time I required transport, Mr Gate, my boss, ensured it was available, and for this I thank him and everyone else who supported me at this traumatic time of my life.

Mum, back in Winchester, kept asking to go home, but she required twenty-four-hour attention, so they did the next best thing and asked her if she would like to go to Andover War Memorial Hospital. She agreed readily.

One night I went to the Christmas play at Castledown School. The play finished and the audience commenced to leave the theatre. Standing in the foyer were two friends of Mum's, Gordon and Margaret Willem.

"Come on, John," they said. "We'll take you to your mum. She's had a turn for the worse."

We arrived. The staff nurse asked me to go to my mother immediately. Mum's breathing was laboured.

I said, "Calm down, calm down."

She seemed to relax a bit. At exactly 10 p.m., no more than a couple of minutes after I arrived, she drew her last breath.

I said to her, "I love you, Mum. I love you."

Margaret and Gordon left us alone.

I kissed her forehead and placed the sheet over her face. I stayed for about five minutes or so, saying silly things like "Be good in heaven" and "Wait for me".

This was 10 December 1984. God, how I miss her!

My two sisters and my brother had to be informed. I contacted Gail and Michaela. My brother was a different kettle of fish. He was at this time a guest of Her Majesty in Leicester Prison, and I just could not contact him. Social services were contacted, and they assisted me to organise the funeral. Mum's body was taken to the chapel of rest close to the Andover church so that friends and members of the family could pay their last respects.

My grandfather and my two sisters arrived. No one seemed to know whether my brother had been informed or not.

I contacted the crematorium, and they organised the funeral with the vicar's help. Mum's will stated that she wished to be cremated, then her ashes buried in Ludgershall Churchyard with her maiden name, Richardson, on the memorial stone. All of this meant a great deal of organisation, and I will always be grateful to social services for their assistance during these difficult times.

The strangest thing of all is I can never remember actually crying, but I remember vividly the tremendous hurt I felt inside – a tearing, wrenching hurt that I still feel and, I suppose, always will feel when I think of my mother and what she must have gone through.

After the cremation and the interment of Mum's ashes, everyone assembled at Mum's house for some refreshments and to show our last respects.

I had to contact the council with regard to transferring the house to my name. This was done.

The real pain and sense of loss began to encompass me. I was alone in Mum's house – now transferred to me. I had the sorrowful task of getting Mum's belongings out of the house. My sisters shared her jewellery and helped me with her personal effects. I changed Mum's bedding and decided to use her bed. I used to lie in bed cuddling her pillow to me and speaking to her, hoping she would hear me. Sometimes I thought I was going mad. I felt so alone. I guess this was my way of grieving. I just could not accept that she was no longer there; I felt her presence in the house and just kept talking as though she was there. I could not really accept that she was dead.

I now regretted deeply the times I argued with her, and the times I upset her. I realised that I must have caused her a great deal of pain, and I could not come to terms with this.

Here I was reverting to the old pattern: up to my eyes in debts, rent, rates, electricity bills and water bills and feeling very sorry for myself. I knew my mother would have disapproved of this, so I began to think of ways to get myself out of this awful rut.

At this time, I asked for and received some good sound advice from my colleagues – in particular Mr Gates. He was always very helpful, and for this I thank him.

Mum's will quite rightly divided her assets equally in four – each of her children to receive one-quarter of any money that was left. Mum did have some hire-purchase agreements, and I am afraid that the quarter share I received did not cover the debts I had. I never mentioned this to my family because I wanted mother's wishes to be carried out exactly as she requested. Anyway, I was left the house and furniture, so I had a lot to be thankful for.

Another friend who helped me through these difficult times was Janette. I had known her for quite some time and considered her one of my best friends. Janette is deaf, and we used to communicate using sign language. This was marvellous as no one else knew what we were talking about. At this time Janette was a bit of a tomboy – short hair, trousers, jeans.

One day I asked her if she would like to accompany me to a disco at the sports club. I suggested that she should wear a dress and try to look a bit more feminine. She took a great deal of persuading, but finally she agreed.

Janette arrived and knocked on my door. I opened it and couldn't believe my eyes – dress, make-up, the lot. She looked lovely, and I told her so.

When we arrived at the sports club she was greeted by

wolf whistles. She had never been whistled at before and was embarrassed, blushing quite profusely. How sweet she looked! I put a protective arm around her. I reckon I was like a brother to her, and I wanted to ensure no harm came to her. The other guys must have sensed this, and they left us alone.

The evening was most enjoyable. Janette said she had a super time. At the end of the disco her parents, who were also very protective, arrived to take her home in their car.

The following day she turned up in her jeans again. The disappointment must have shown on my face, because she asked me what was wrong. I told her I preferred her to act and dress like a young woman. Eventually, after a lot of badgering and coaxing, she took heed and gradually changed her mode of dress and behaviour. We were now going out on a regular basis, but only as friends. Janette told me she was looking for a boyfriend, and I tried to advise her on her choice. There were times when I thought of Janette as my girlfriend, but she never gave any indication that she thought of me in the same way. I always felt that her parents had advised her against it. I also felt her parents never understood how I felt, so I never really pursued it. Another reason her parents may have disapproved of me was the occasion we were both invited to a wedding party in the Memorial Hall.

Janette was under age for drinking, but, as many young people do, she insisted on trying a few, and I did not realise either how strong the drink was or how many she had. She was fine until we stepped outside into the fresh air. She collapsed and I fell on top of her.

I eventually managed to pick her up, just as a police car was passing. I held Janette as though I was kissing her, and they just drove on. She was absolutely dead drunk, and I draped her over my shoulder and tried to carry her home. Of course I had been drinking as well, and I was now staggering all over the place. I fell twice, but, fortunately for Janette's sake, she landed on me, which cushioned her fall.

We arrived at the door, having been assisted by a kind passer-by. I fumbled for the key, simultaneously trying to prevent Janette from sliding down the wall. This was extremely difficult. At last I managed to get her to the settee and made her as comfortable as possible. She came round and asked for a basin. She was very ill! Somehow she made it known to me that she wanted her father to pick her up.

Her father arrived. To say he was angry is the understatement of the century. He was stark raving mad – and of course had every right to be. She was under age and he held me responsible. He stormed off, making it quite clear I should not see Janette again.

The following morning Janette explained the situation to her parents, and this apparently calmed her father down. Janette's mother telephoned me and asked me to go up to their home and see them. Janette had been very ill all night. She had, though, persuaded her father that her condition had not been my fault. Nevertheless, I kept apologising. I felt as guilty as hell. My apologies were accepted, but somehow our relationship was never the same. We remain good friends, and I hope and trust we always will be.

I always had the impression that Janette's father did like me but purely as a friend for his daughter. He did allow me to continue our friendship. In other words, her parents made it quite clear they did not mind us being friends, but nothing more.

CHAPTER X

THE 1985 LONDON MARATHON

During all of this, I was still thinking deeply about the London Marathon. I was committed to doing the run. My mother had known this and had been very, very concerned for me. My grief at my mother's death was overwhelming, but through all of this I knew that I would have to continue training. The thought of not attempting the marathon or stopping my training, strangely enough, never ever entered my mind. It was a deep-rooted commitment. I just had to go through with it.

I was now living by myself, and trying to come to terms with all that this involved. Apart from getting myself up and ready for work, there was the cleaning, washing, ironing, shopping and so on. Oh, my God, how I had taken all of this for granted! Frustration, depression and anxiety at times overwhelmed me, but they simultaneously spurred me on to train harder and harder. I felt that I now had no choice. I drove myself harder and harder, the tears and the sweat mingling as I plodded on and on, driving, driving, trying to run the grief out of myself. No one will ever know how terribly lost and alone I felt, but through all of this I was determined to train as hard as I could. Perhaps this was my salvation – who knows?'

The date of the London Marathon – 21 April 1985 – was only a few weeks away, and I was beginning to look forward to the event when I had a horrendous setback.

At lunchtime at work we used to play football on a concrete hardstanding. One day I accidentally trod on a metal bolt and fell. There was a resounding crack as my hip came into contact with the concrete. I thought I might have broken it – one always thinks the worst on these occasions!

I was taken to the surgery, where I was examined by Dr Wells. He knew about my commitment to the marathon and was very worried. The bad news was that I could not run under any circumstances for the time being.

What a bloody quandary I was in. Many good, kind people had sponsored me, and some had already paid their money in good faith. What was I going to do? What was I going to tell them? I felt so stupid that I had placed myself in a position where there was the remotest chance of injury. There was little doubt my leg was badly damaged, but with about a fortnight to go before the marathon I just had to try to loosen up and get on with it.

I got into my tracksuit and set off – limp, plod, limp, plod. The pain was excruciating. Eventually I could bear it no longer and had to ring for a taxi to take me home. I had no cash with me, but the driver agreed to take me home and be paid on arrival. I hobbled into the house, then back to the taxi and paid the driver.

God, I cannot remember ever experiencing pain like that. I decided to run a hot bath – as hot as I could stand it. I lowered myself into the searing liquid and just lay there groaning for what seemed ages. It must have been a long time: the water was barely tepid when I dragged my aching body out of it and sank into a chair.

I couldn't really train as I was supposed to. This added to my doubts, fears and worry. All I could do was very light exercise and try to stay as loose as possible. On Friday 19 April I had a long discussion with a friend of mine. He asked me how I felt and he suggested I give my leg a little trial jog. I did; it felt decidedly better, but still painful. He encouraged me to at least get to the starting point and see how I felt when the race started.

He thought that once I got warmed up the muscles would ease and I would feel better. I listened to him intently and made the decision to go. I could not, under any circumstances, let the good people of Ludgershall, my sponsors and, above all, my mother down. I felt Mum very close to me now, and I believed that she would help to see me through.

We arrived in London and, after a great deal of hassle, found somewhere to stay the night before the marathon.

The London Marathon starts at Blackheath. There were two starting points – Red and Blue. This, I guess, is to avoid congestion. I was at the Red start.

There were some very distinguished marathon runners there that day. Steve Jones, who was twenty-nine at the time and a corporal in the RAF, was competing alongside Ingrid Kristiansen of Norway – one of the greatest female marathon runners of all time. Behind them came every variety of the human race, from the extremely fit and healthy to people like Linda Down, a twenty-eight-year-old American woman who suffers from cerebral palsy. Despite this, Linda compels herself over the 26.2-mile course on crutches. Why does she do it? Because, she says, she wants to be part of the human race instead of being regarded with pity for her terrible disability. I guess this is what compelled me to prove myself as well. We, 'the handicapped', do not want pity; we want understanding and assistance to help us overcome our disabilities.

One man, Phil Bray of Orpington (No. 8008) competed in the Rotterdam Marathon on Saturday the 20th, caught the overnight ferry and arrived in London ready to start the London Marathon. Another man, Martyn Ridgers (No. 5603) was married at 3.30 p.m. on Saturday at St Michael's, Aldershot and at 5.30 a.m. on Sunday he left his nuptial bed to spend the first day of his honeymoon running around London.

Also many great characters get involved in fancy dress – William Shakespeare, Halley's Comet, a seven-foot-six mouse and Ursula Andress (a runner clad in a minute bikini). Dale Lyons (No. V985) dressed as a chef and attempted a pancake-flipping record.

Then there are the people who really touch your heart: the blind runners strapped to their seeing partners; people suffering from multiple sclerosis; Kathy Robotham from Muswell Hill (No. F753), who is mentally handicapped; Jeremy Pye from High Wycombe (No. C300). Bob Wiseman eighty-two years young (No. T993) was the oldest man, and Carla Ali of Regents Park, London (No. P330) was the oldest lady.

My number was R995.

It's amazing the boost it gave me when I saw so many people far, far worse off than myself. I was going to do this and I was doing it for Mum and all my good friends and the people of Ludgershall.

When the usual preliminaries were over – belongings placed in a black plastic bag, labelled and stored in a place of safety until the end of the marathon – a fellow came up to me and enquired whether this was my first time.

I said, "It is my first London Marathon and I'm worried about my leg."

He said, "Don't worry. Just jog along for a couple of miles; soak up the atmosphere. You'll soon forget your pain."

I certainly hoped he was right.

The atmosphere was tremendous. Everyone was shaking hands. Old friends were embracing, wishing each other luck. Thousands of people were shouting encouragement.

The spectators may not realise this, but they also play a very important part; in fact, their encouragement and cheerful banter soon makes the participants forget the enormity of the task ahead. I was becoming more and more excited, and, at the same time, a feeling of well-being and relaxation came over me. I felt good. I decided to take my colleague's advice and take it very easy for the first few miles.

The start gun fired. We were off! I felt no pain. The adrenaline was flowing. I felt relaxed and very confident. Mum's face was in my mind all of this time, and I thought of my sponsors at home.

'Mum, this is for you. I am doing this for you,' I thought.

I started to run faster and faster, and I had to control myself. I had a long, long way to go. I remembered the lessons I had learned in the past, when I tired myself out prematurely – so steady, boy, steady! Plod on, plod on!

I must have been about halfway when my legs became numb. I just could not feel them. God, I felt miserable! All the promises I had made myself, all the people who had sponsored me! I staggered a bit, walked a bit, ran a bit. I was really just moving by instinct. I told myself to keep going. I could feel the blisters on my feet again, and the squelch, squelch of the blood and sweat between my toes.

A woman came up alongside. "Follow me," she said. "Follow me. Keep up with me. We're nearly at Tower Bridge. There's only a few miles. Come on, come on – you can do it."

Whoever she was, she was an inspiration. I just gazed at her back and blindly followed. My heart felt dead. Tears mingled with the sweat that ran in rivulets down my face. God, I was in a state! I thought of my mother.

I kept repeating to myself, "Mum, Mum, I'm nearly home. I'll do it, I'll do it!"

Plod, plod, squelch, squelch, went my aching feet.

"We're nearly there," my escort informed me. Keep going, keep going."

I looked up through a mist of sweat and tears. I could see Westminster Bridge, and I knew that when we crossed that we were nearly there. I just kept going. I had to finish now.

I cannot really remember much except when I staggered across the finish line someone plonked a Mars Bar in my hand and placed a silver-foil cape over my shoulders. I remember a very attractive girl came forward, kissed me and placed a medal over my head. I felt so proud, and I thought of how Mum would have felt had she been there.

My mind went blank. Apparently I passed out. Later I was informed that I had been placed on a stretcher and taken to a hospital for a check-up. My feet were covered in blisters; the blisters had burst and my socks were soaked with blood and had to be cut off to enable my feet to be examined. I had no feeling in my damaged leg whatsoever. After dressing my wounds, two nurses spent some time trying to get me walking again.

Yes, I, John Hall of Ludgershall, severely handicapped, had completed the London Marathon. It would not sink in. I just could not believe it. What a day! What a glorious bloody day!

I cannot remember much about the journey home; I was on such a high. I could not believe that I had completed the London Marathon.

I do remember, though, the feeling of utter exhaustion and the great difficulty I experienced when walking – the task of placing one leg in front of another and trying to spare my blistered aching feet every time they came into contact with the ground.

I do remember the tremendous welcome home I received from my good friends and neighbours in Ludgershall. There was a large notice on the door: 'Welcome Home, John. Well Done.' The cheering and applause all round somewhat overwhelmed me, and I felt tears running down my cheeks. They were tears of happiness. I learned later that Tom and Barbara Humphries were mainly responsible for the welcoming committee, and for this I thank them; it made all the blood, sweat and tears seem worth it, and helped me to restore my confidence and faith in myself.

I also remember the numerous steaming baths, trying to relieve the aches and pains, and gingerly walking downstairs one step at a time. The leg I had injured at football prior to the marathon did not seem to belong to me at all.

Everywhere I went in the village and at work, people were congratulating me, patting me on the back. "Well done!" "Good on you, mate!" and "How the hell did you manage it?" were some of the greetings.

A fortnight after the marathon I still ached and my feet were still blistered.

Of course, they were going to take a long time to heal properly. I also learned that Tom and Barbara had video'd the marathon for me, and this is now one of my prize possessions.

I had the task of collecting the rest of my sponsorship money, and the *Andover Advertiser* reporters and photographers were there when Lloyds Bank presented me with a cheque. Altogether I collected £500, which eventually was presented to Mencap, the charity for the mentally handicapped.

The people at work were tremendous. Mr Gate, my boss, presented me with a tankard that my workmates had a collection for, and the major general in charge of the vehicle depot asked to meet me personally so that he could shake my hand and see the medal presented for completing the marathon.

The reporters visited again and asked if I had any plans for the future.

Without really thinking, I said, "Oh yes, my next goal is the New York Marathon in 1986."

I had not even thought about finances, sponsorship or anything, and there I was already putting my big foot in it. Here we go again, John – blabbing off! Commit yourself first and everything else will follow!

CHAPTER XI

THE 1986 NEW YORK MARATHON

A couple of months after the London Marathon I started to feel like training again and, with the New York Marathon as my next target, I started to get back into the swing of things.

The following is an extract from a write-up in the local newspaper:

Marathon Man Off to the States

Ludgershall's Marathon Man, John Hall, is to fly to America to take part in the New York Marathon. For thirty-one year old John, who lives at Old Common Way, Ludgershall, running has provided a way to beat his physical and mental disabilities. He will be taking the good wishes of all his neighbours plus those of his workmates at the Vehicle Depot, Ludgershall, when he tackles his second long distance run. John said he is fit and ready to go. "I am looking forward to the marathon in America" he continued "It's all going to be a totally new experience for me."

I decided to work out a training programme for myself. The good people who sponsored me for the London Marathon were prepared to sponsor me again. They ran discos in the Memorial Hall, and, with other fund-raising activities, managed to raise quite a sum of money. The balance was provided by John Vidal, the man who owned the video shop. He paid for my fare and accommodation, and for this I will be eternally grateful.

The rules for the New York Marathon are slightly different to those for the London Marathon. I merely responded to a magazine advertisement giving my name and address, paid my dues and was automatically booked in.

The details arrived in the post and I was all set to go. My number was C647.

I found the flight most exciting. I requested to see the cockpit and was taken there by a gorgeous stewardess. The aircraft was a Boeing 747, and I was amazed at the number of dials and levers. What a responsibility pilots have! We do take a lot for granted, don't we?

The pilot asked me why I was going to New York, and, when I told him, he announced it over the intercom. With the usual American flair for exaggeration, he said that I was representing Great Britain in the New York Marathon. When I returned to my seat I was greeted with loud cheers and applause, and children surrounded me, asking for my autograph. God, I did feel important! Everyone wanted to shake my hand or pat me on the back and wish me good luck. Americans just love making a fuss and I thoroughly enjoyed it.

We arrived at John F. Kennedy Airport. I remember it was a Tuesday and very, very cold. At Airport Arrivals we were directed towards the immigration area as aliens. I remember laughing at this and joking with my fellow passengers about landing from Mars. At last a charming young lady looked at my passport, stamped it and asked me what I was doing in New York. I told her. She wished me good luck and I was through – I had passed the aliens test.

I hailed a Yellow Cab and told the driver to take me to the hotel that had been booked. I can't for the life of me remember either what it was called or where in New York it was, but eventually we arrived.

I was shown my room, which I was sharing to cut costs. Then as I was starting to feel hungry I left my bag on my bed and went out to look for somewhere to eat.

I'll never forget the impact. There were people everywhere, scurrying about like ants. Car horns were continually beeping, police and ambulance sirens were wailing – the hustle and bustle was overwhelming. This place was *alive*. I felt a bit apprehensive walking around by myself.

Ah, a familiar sight – McDonald's! They seem to be everywhere – a little bit of familiarity regardless of where you go in the world. Good old McDonald's! I went in and had something to eat. I returned to the hotel very tired, and

I wanted to get to bed as soon as possible. I knew that the following day we were to be picked up by coach and given a tour of the course. The start was near the Statue of Liberty.

On the day of the marathon I rose early, ate a good breakfast and checked through my bag to ensure I had my equipment. I got ready for the race, resplendent in Union Jack vest and shorts. I was so proud to be British – and yes, in a way I *was* representing the handicapped people of Great Britain. I felt good. I pulled on my tracksuit, made sure my bag was labelled, and waited for the transport to take us to the starting point.

We arrived by coach near the start. I can't remember much about individuals or anything; I was in a bit of a dreamlike state. I could not believe that I was in New York, about to start my second marathon. What I do remember, though, is that it was very, very cold. I had forgotten my T-shirt and had only my vest and shorts.

At last we lined up. There didn't appear to be as many taking part as in the London Marathon, but there appeared to be millions of spectators.

The gun fired – we were off across a bridge that seemed to vibrate as the runners made their way across it. It did run through my mind that it could collapse, but of course it didn't. I could see TV cameras everywhere, and the crowds waving and cheering all the way. I felt brilliant, confident, fit – a far cry from my first effort in Ludgershall. I just followed the main body of runners on and on through the Jewish area into the heart of New York. Although my feet and legs were aching slightly, I was not experiencing the 'splidge, splodge' of blood and sweat. I put this down to the fact that it was so bloody cold that my feet had not reached sweating temperature. Yes, I felt good in this run.

In what seemed like no time at all I could see the finish line, and I had not experienced any major problems at all.

At the finish we went through the now familiar procedures: being wrapped in foil to maintain body heat (that's a laugh), then we were presented with our medals and congratulated and kissed. I was getting quite used to this – and yes, I did enjoy it, every minute of it. It was a wonderful experience.

That evening there was a reception and party for all

participants. Quite a number of professional runners were there, including some from Brazil, Africa and Australia, and at least two from New York. A couple of professionals sat at our table and, of course, running dominated the conversation. They were all amazed that I had taken part and were full of praise and admiration for my efforts.

It was a typical American party, full of razzmatazz, prize-giving, speeches, thousands of balloons, flags, etc. It was a great and memorable evening – but, God, I was absolutely knackered! I was looking forward to a couple of days sightseeing before I flew home.

I decided to go back to the hotel and go to bed. I remember drifting off, listening to the continuous wail of sirens.

The following day I explored New York. A friend and I went into Central Park in the afternoon and took some photographs. I persuaded two policemen to have a picture taken with me. One handcuffed me and said, "Sorry, sir, you're breaking the law." I didn't know whether to take him seriously, but his face broke into a broad grin and I thanked God he was only joking. They really had me going for a moment.

I was amazed at the speed which the lift went to the top of the Empire State Building. The view from the top is breathtaking. People on the streets resembled ants scurrying to and fro, and cars looked like Dinky Toys.

I spent the third day travelling around on the Underground. The trains and carriages are literally covered in graffiti – some of it quite artistic, but, on the whole, messy. It is a great pity that all the artistic qualities and energy spent in graffiti cannot be channelled into more useful pursuits.

We boarded a boat to Manhattan to visit the Statue of Liberty, and we viewed the old torch that had recently been replaced. A spiral staircase led to the top and gave us a good view of Manhattan Bridge.

That evening we ventured through some of the backstreets of Manhattan, and I was shocked and amazed when I nearly tripped over a very beautiful young woman lying on the pavement. Apparently "the broad had overdosed". By the time the ambulance arrived, she was dead. I thought of the continuous sirens and realised that something like this could have happened every time I heard one – drugs overdoses, murders, rapes, someone lying in some dingy backstreet breathing their last. A shudder ran through me!

I must say, there were some very attractive young ladies of the night strolling around. I admired them from a distance.

Alas, the time came to board the 747 for home! I settled in the aircraft and felt really happy and content. I had achieved what I had set out to do – the Big Double – London and New York!

I was very, very tired when I eventually arrived back in England. The aircraft had been diverted to Gatwick, which meant a long delay getting picked up.

The now familiar pattern evolved: everyone congratulating me, children queuing to see my medal. In fact, this went on for months. Yes, I was once again something of a local hero.

The following write-up in the local newspaper just about sums it up:

Jet Set John's At the Double

John Hall, a 30 year old suffering from acute spasticity has notched up a remarkable double, after completing the gruelling New York Marathon.

John of Old Common Way Ludgershall, who last year pounded his way to success in the London Marathon, is now one of the few disabled people to achieve the dream double. His burning ambition since starting to run five years ago.

Despite his physical disability, John, who smilingly boasts "I run better than I walk" completed the 26-mile New York Marathon in five hours. Villagers rallied round John (whose sponsored run was in aid of Mencap) in his determination to run in America. His airfare was paid by a local businessman and other expenses were met by donations from village traders and Andover Lions Club and proceeds from a local dance in the village hall.

When John arrived home on Wednesday he was given an enthusiastic welcome by villagers.

Said a Councillor "it was a marvellous achievement and we are all very proud of him!"

When asked what my next target was I automatically, and without much forethought, blurted out, "The Berlin Marathon, of course."

CHAPTER XII

THE 1987 BERLIN MARATHON

I was informed that I should apply to take part in the Berlin Marathon via the *Runner's World* magazine. I decided that this time I would run for a particular hospital and, recalling my visits to Winchester Hospital during my mother's illness, I thought I would attempt to raise funds for Winchester Hospital. Thereby, in some small way perhaps, I hoped to repay some of the kindness shown to my mother and our family during my mother's illness.

I rang the hospital and established who their fund-raising officer was. He seemed extremely interested and suggested that we arrange a meeting. Prior to this meeting I prepared a dossier of the marathons I had already completed, and of course I had photographs and my medals as proof of actually taking part. It was decided at the meeting that the fund-raising officer would organise fêtes and other events to raise funds to cover my airfare, accommodation, etc., whilst I would organise sponsorship to repay this and, with luck, earn some capital towards hospital funds.

Time passed quickly, as always with work and training. About a fortnight before the marathon was due I rang the fund-raising officer. He assured me there was nothing to worry about. He said my flight and accommodation were in hand, and that he would be contacting me soon with details.

Time passed by and, with three days to go, I telephoned Winchester Hospital. My frustration and concern must have been obvious.

He kept saying, "Don't panic, don't panic. Your tickets will be at the Tidworth Holiday Company in plenty of time."

The following day, with two days to go, I went to the

Tidworth Holiday Company office as advised.

"Yes," they said, "we have the flight tickets, but nothing has been said about arranging accommodation."

I felt really frustrated, worried and completely let down. Here I was with flight tickets to Berlin, no accommodation organised and not a penny in my pocket.

I knew that if I withdrew money from my bank account, I would be overdrawn, but I had no option. I had to have money to cover expenses. I had no idea what I was going to do about accommodation, but I could not let my sponsors and friends in Ludgershall down. I had to go, even if I had to sleep rough. Needless to say, I was extremely disappointed with my friend the fund-raising 'expert' from Winchester Hospital.

The day of the flight arrived. I travelled in the train to London, then to Heathrow – all at my own expense, of course. I was now getting quite used to airport boarding procedures and quickly found myself on board the Dan-Air flight to Berlin. I was seated next to an elderly lady. Nothing was said for quite some time.

She broke the silence: "You are not looking very happy, young man," she said. "Vot is troublink you?"

I explained my predicament to her – the fact that I was taking part in the Berlin Marathon and accommodation had not been arranged as promised.

"Do not vorry yourself," she said. "I live in Berlin. I luff marathon runners. You must come and liff mit me. You vill be my own marathon runner. I vill keep you. You must meet my family."

I could not believe my luck. Here was a very kind elderly lady willing to accommodate a complete stranger in her own home for the duration of the marathon. Yes, someone up there must be looking after me! My guardian angel was working overtime!

Once we were engaged in conversation, the flight seemed to take about five minutes.

"Fasten your seat belts please. No smoking. We are about to land."

She really fussed over me like a mother hen.

"Come, come," she said. "My son vill be here mit the car."

Her son was there. I wondered what sort of reception he would give an English handicapped marathon runner, but he was utterly charming. He guided us both towards his car and then transported us to their flat – somewhere in Berlin. Don't ask me where; I haven't a clue. On entering the flat I was introduced to his wife. She didn't speak English and was obviously expecting a baby. I apologised to her for my intrusion, but my apologies were brushed aside. They were all so very kind.

I felt extremely hungry by this time, and also very embarrassed. I offered to pay some money towards my food and accommodation, but they would not hear of it.

After we ate we sat and talked for quite some time. The son contacted a friend who was in the car business, and he arranged that I should be collected and transported to his mother's, where she had a spare room. The mother's English was limited so (bearing in mind my speech impediment and hearing difficulties) I tried to explain to her son what I wanted translating to his mother. I can assure you it was very embarrassing for all concerned.

After two nights, most of which we spent in awkward silence, I asked the son if he could possibly find me accommodation near the town centre as I had been informed this was where the marathon would start. The fellow was very understanding; he understood the predicament I was in.

I asked him to thank his mother for the kindness she had shown me and apologised for my lack of knowledge of her native language. She hugged me and we left.

I was transported to somewhere in the middle of Berlin. I didn't have a clue where we were. It turned out we were somewhere in the red-light district at a home for the elderly run by one of the son's friends – and, incidentally, it was situated above a brothel. The embarrassment I felt was balanced by the low cost of the room.

I decided to have a walk round the immediate area and took note of street names, building names and so on, so that if I got lost, at least I would have some information regarding where I wanted to get back to. I bought a map of Berlin and decided to research where the marathon main office and start point were. Of course no one understood what the hell I was on about, and I got some peculiar looks, I can tell you.

At last, a bit of luck! I was passing a telephone kiosk and heard a woman speaking in English. I waited till she finished her conversation; then I approached her.

"Excuse me, madam," I said, trying to assuage her anxiety. "Could you possibly direct me to the Berlin Marathon Office, or ask someone where it is. I am afraid my German is non-existent. This is my first visit to Berlin."

She indicated that she was in a hurry but would try.

She approached a German chap and he gave her the directions, which she transferred to me. Apparently it all happened in the heart of Berlin.

At last I found the office, and I was given my number (3122) and confirmation badge. I was officially registered. I now had the information I required. Marathons are basically the same, when all is said and done. All you need to know is (a) starting point, (b) start time, (c) route and (d) finish line. Easy, isn't it? The only problem is the twenty-six gruelling miles in between (a) and (d)!

I now concentrated on visiting places of interest in Berlin: the Chinese Garden, Checkpoint Charlie, the Wall, the bunker where Hitler supposedly committed suicide, and the government building. What impressed me most of all was the cleanliness of the streets. There was not a bit of paper or a matchstick anywhere to be seen. Even on market days apparently the streets are spotless about half an hour after completion of business.

The day prior to the marathon, I took part in what is known as the Kingston Breakfast Run. I set off about 6 a.m. and headed for the Olympic Stadium, where I had breakfast with some of the other participants. Around the walls were some names of famous athletes who had performed here: Jesse Owens, Sebastian Coe and many others.

I met a charming couple who were stationed in Germany and had at one time been stationed at Tidworth Garrison, about two miles from Ludgershall. We had a long chat and I found myself wishing I had met them earlier. They were living in a caravan parked not too far from the stadium, and they had spare accommodation.

On the day of the marathon, 4 October 1987, I rose early, checked my equipment, had a light breakfast, then headed towards the starting point. Even at this early hour the sun was beating down and it was very, very warm. 'God knows what it is going to be like as the day wears on!' I thought.

We all bunched up waiting for the start gun. Then we were off. My thoughts, as always, turned to home and to my sponsors – the many kind people in Ludgershall and elsewhere who had encouraged me. I also thought of Winchester Hospital, the charity for which I was running.

I decided to take things easy at first – just gently plod on – but the ground seemed very flat and I began to accelerate. I had never felt so good. I felt as though I could run for ever. The only thing that worried me was the tremendous heat. God bless the members of the German fire brigade who decided to shower us with cold water about halfway round. It was refreshing and broke the monotony.

I plodded on and on, following everyone else, passing the photograph checkpoints, onwards, onwards. I could not believe how quickly the distance seemed to pass. Before I knew where I was I could see the finish line, and I still felt as fresh as a daisy.

I crossed the finish line amidst thunderous applause and was again embraced by a most charming young lady. She placed the medal around my neck and kissed me.

I just continued to walk, gradually coming down from the tremendous high feeling I always got when I successfully completed a marathon. It really is a wonderful feeling to have the medal round my neck, with all the passers-by applauding, patting me on the back, smiling and laughing, full of goodwill. It was wonderful.

I gradually cooled off and calmed down. My thoughts turned to getting back to my lodgings, having a shower, getting changed and going out on the town. This was a new feeling for me. I was usually too knackered to do anything after a marathon. This must prove something: I had reached a fair level of fitness.

Of course there was a damper: I had only a limited amount of cash left. I had budgeted to the best of my ability, but I also had to think of the journey home. I had to content myself with a pizza and a beer. Ah well, perhaps it was a blessing in disguise. I might have been tempted in other less desirable directions if I had plenty of cash, bearing in mind the area in which I was residing. Who knows!

The important thing of course was that I had completed another Big One – the Berlin Marathon. I was a very happy chappie.

I am sorry that I did not contact my elderly benefactor or any of the good, kind people who helped me in Berlin, but I would like to record here my heartfelt thanks to all of them. I will always have very happy memories of that trip to Berlin – in particular, their concern and kindness with regard to my welfare.

I don't recall very much about the flight home. I slept most of the way. I remember dreaming vividly about the exquisite creature who had presented my medal to me. Perhaps this was the real reason I took part in the marathons – the kiss and the embrace at the finish. Well, could be!

It was all routine now: touch down at Heathrow, travel across London to Waterloo, then catch the train to Andover where, hopefully, there would be a bus for Ludgershall.

Once again I was stony broke, but I had achieved what I had set out to do.

My joy was short-lived. There was a brown envelope from my bank manager inside the front door requesting my presence in his office to discuss my overdraft. Ah well, I can't say it was unexpected.

The following morning everywhere I went I was warmly congratulated, and I was invited to Winchester Hospital for a presentation. I wondered if I would see my fund-raising officer when I presented the cheque to their charity. I did not mention the fact that for the last month or so I had been living on tinned soup in an attempt to pay off my overdraft.

The *Andover Advertiser*, 4 March 1988, reported:

John Hall, a disabled marathon runner of Old Common Way Ludgershall, handed over a cheque for £450 to Sister Jill Diamond and Ray Allen of the Royal Hampshire County Hospital Medical Fund at Winchester. The money was raised after John completed last year's Berlin Marathon.

Earlier, on 8 January 1988, they had reported:

Ludgershall's marathon runner, John Hall, was at Boscombe Down recently to receive a gift from an Andover Club. John has ignored physical and mental handicaps to take part in The London and New York Marathons to raise money for charities associated with Mencap.

He is also Chairman of the Andover Deaf Club and is shown receiving a computer, printer and monitor, bought after wives at the Aeroplane and Armament Experimental Depot made a profit of £1,000 from thrift shop sales. The wives decided to aid the local Deaf Club and the equipment will be put to good use producing a newsletter for the club. John expressed his sincere thanks to Mrs Maggie Glover and all the wives who had been involved.

Unfortunately, the Andover Deaf Club has since ceased to exist, mainly through lack of interest on the part of members, and it remains a mystery what happened to the computer and other equipment.

The next couple of years I spent just getting on with my life, but still keeping fit. I felt as though I had achieved what I had set out to do – to prove to myself and others that the handicapped have ambitions, hopes and dreams. I did think of raising more money for charity, but felt that I needed time to stabilise my own finances, in particular the losses I had accrued during the Berlin Marathon.

CHAPTER XIII

THE 1990 LONDON MARATHON

Early in 1989 I began to get itchy feet. I was decidedly bored. 'Yes,' I thought, 'it's time to have another crack at the London Marathon.'

This time applications had to be made through the Trustee Savings Bank. I applied, and I received confirmation that I had been accepted. My number was 14236.

As previously stated, my general fitness was pretty good. I was also involved at this time in disco-dancing sessions two or three times a week. This by itself keeps you fit – a form of aerobics, I guess.

I entered the marathon as a member of Harry Carpenter's team, and we were to be known as the Rupert Bear Team. We were running in aid of people suffering from muscular dystrophy.

The marathon was in April, so that gave me time to find sponsors. By this time I had become very friendly with a chap called Steve Diamond. He offered to assist me in organising accommodation, transport and so on during our stay in London. I must say it was a great boost to my morale to have a friend in my corner, so to speak, and for this support I would like to thank him.

The day of the marathon dawned. I hadn't slept very well. I drew back the curtains and peered out. My God, it was raining! I've never witnessed rain like it. The drains could not cope. There must have been a couple of inches of water running down the street. 'Not an ideal day for running twenty-six miles!' I thought. 'Never mind – it may clear up by the off.'

But it did not. It just kept on pouring down. We had breakfast, Steve and I, then he organised our transport to take us to the Red start at Greenwich Park. The virgin runners (new people) would leave from the Blue start at Shooters Hill. Apparently it was the poorest turnout ever for a London Marathon, but, as always, there were thousands and thousands of spectators.

The rain did not let up. It was one of those situations where you just accept the conditions and get on with it. We were all soaked to the skin before the start. One comedian started singing 'Singing in the Rain' and sploshing about in the numerous puddles. Before we knew what was going on we were all at it – about 11,000 Gene Kellys minus the umbrellas. It's a wonder we heard the start gun. Apparently they had thought about abandoning the marathon; but fortunately they didn't, and once again we were off. Never mind – just twenty-six miles to go.

The atmosphere was tremendous. There's something about us Brits: the more horrible the conditions, the more the spectators seem determined to enjoy themselves. I have never known such enthusiasm! It could have been because of the reduced number of participants, but it seemed as though the cheering and encouragement was more personal. Yes, they seemed to be cheering for me personally.

Oh, God, what a day! Plod, splosh, plod, splosh, onward, onward, plod, splosh. I began to feel decidedly sorry for myself. I could feel my feet getting very wet indeed. 'Here we go again,' I thought: wet socks lubricating my feet, sliding inside my trainers, and bloody, red-raw blisters. God, I must be bonkers!

Feeling sorry for myself soon passed, though; I started to think positively. I thought of Mum, as always; I thought of Sebastian Coe (my hero) – would he give up? Would he hell! My sponsors – I could not let them down. Plod, splosh, plod, splosh. If only it hadn't been raining! Ah well, it is, so let's get on with it.

At last I reached the finish line, and I went through the by now familiar routine: foil, medal, kiss, and cheering, applauding crowds. Steve Diamond was at the finish. He practically carried me to the taxi rank, and then had to support me to the hotel and all the way to my room. When we eventually arrived at Waterloo he literally had to lift my legs one by one on to the train whilst I hung round his neck. When we were on the train to Andover he tried to massage some life back into my limbs, but to no avail.

We arrived home and a chap who was lodging with me at the time had stretched a banner across the window: 'Well Done. Congratulations." And dear Tom and Barbara Humphries from next door cracked open a bottle of champers – this was becoming a habit.

A few weeks passed and I received a phone call. I had been nominated for a special award.

The following extract from a report by John Anderson in the *Andover Advertiser* explains:

Unsung Hero John to Collect His Award

A 34-YEAR-OLD handicapped man, who has raised thousands of pounds for the disabled by running in marathons, is to receive an Unsung Hero award in London next month.

The Celebrities Guild, which makes the annual awards, says that John Hall, of Old Common Way, Ludgershall, near Andover, "displays self-effacing determination, outstanding courage in the face of great adversity and has a warm interest in those worse off than himself."

John . . . has run in four marathons – London twice, Berlin and New York – and he hopes to take part in the London event again next year.

[John] has had to overcome physical handicaps faced by few if any of the competitors in these events.

John . . . in fact [suffers from spasticity]. He was born with a twisted leg, deaf and with [a speech impediment].

He has conquered his deafness, overcome his speech impediment, helped others to master sign language and learned to walk. But, he says: "I can run better than I can walk."

John, who is delighted with the award which will be presented to him at a London hotel on November 4, has raised £5,000 to help the disabled in the last few years. "I couldn't have done it without the help of the people of Ludgershall."

He has lived alone since his mother died five years ago. "Every time I run I think of my mum," he says.

Life has been a tough, uphill struggle for John who first started running when he was 26 and weighing a thumping 17 stones. "I could hardly walk never mind run."

He . . . took part in his first half marathon in 1983, finishing last with bleeding thighs and feet. . . .

[John] has gone back to school to improve his reading, writing and spelling "so that I can then go to college and get some qualifications. I would really like to work in a large organisation helping disabled people."

The following two letters are from Ella Glazer, who was then Honorary Executive Guilder of the Celebrities Guild of Great Britain. In the margin are the names of some of the celebrities who support this charity.

EG/EH/UH90

14 EAST BARNET ROAD
NEW BARNET
HERTS EN4 8RW

Telephone: 081-449 1234
081-449 1515 081-441 2122
(10am-4pm, Weekdays)

19 September 1990

FOUNDER: ELLA GLAZER

Mr J Hall
10 Old Common Way
Ludgershall
Nr Andover
Hants
SP11 9RX

Dear Mr Hall,

It was very nice to speak to you on the telephone and we are delighted that you have been selected and agreed to accept one of our 1990 CELEBRITIES GUILD 'UNSUNG HEROES' AWARDS at our Gala Evening on Sunday, November 4.

As you will see from the enclosed complimentary tickets, our Awards Presentation and Tribute is being held at the Royal Garden Hotel in London's South Kensington, where we shall very much look forward to meeting you.

In order that you may be able to understand what the CELEBRITIES GUILD 'UNSUNG HEROES' AWARDS are all about, I am enclosing a copy of the brochure that was presented to the guests attending the event last year.

We should be most grateful if you could kindly confirm that you will be with us, and if there are any problems please do not hesitate to let us know; e.g. whether you will need help with transport or staying in London overnight, as naturally we shall be happy to be responsible for this.

We are also writing today to the person who nominated you, because we know how delighted they will be that you were selected from several thousand letters of nomination. They too will be invited as guests of the CELEBRITIES GUILD.

We very much look forward to greeting you all.

Yours sincerely,

Ella Glazer

Ella Glazer (Mrs)
Hon Exec. Guilder

P.S. When writing, please could you very kindly let us have a head-and-shoulder photograph of yourself (black and white will be fine). Also could you please tell us the name of your local newspaper, radio station and T.V. company.

Charity Reg. No. 282298

EG/JA

14 EAST BARNET ROAD
NEW BARNET
HERTS EN4 8RW

Telephone: 081-449 1234
081-449 1515 081-441 2122
(10am-4pm, Weekdays)

5 December 1990

Mr J Hall
10 Old Common Way
Ludgershall
Nr Andover
Hants
SP11 9RX

Dear Mr Hall,

During our Gala Evening on November 4, you may remember that Cliff Morgan and I suggested, in passing, that - if you are entering for the London Marathon next year - you might like to do so in aid of the work of the CELEBRITIES GUILD OF GREAT BRITAIN.

We would be delighted if you could do so, and we could certainly provide a celebrity back-up.

Could you please very kindly let me know whether this idea appeals to you so that, with the funds raised, we could provide some more equipment for disabled and handicapped people.

We would need to know very soon because we are currently involved in making arrangements for all sorts of events in 1991, and this would then be included in our calendar.

We would need to discuss with you precisely how you felt we might help you; so perhaps you could very kindly ring me one day here between 10am - 4pm (from Monday to Thursday inclusive).

I hope you got my letter of November 19, as I do not appear to have received a reply to it.

Warmest good wishes.

Yours sincerely,

Ella Glazer (Mrs)
Hon. Exec. Guilder

The day of the award was slightly spoiled by the fact that I had been robbed sometime during the week. This was discovered when I went to the box in which I kept the gold rings and other bits and pieces of jewellery that I wore on special occasions only. The box was empty. I had over the past few weeks given shelter and a home to someone (who shall be nameless) who was down on his luck; he repaid me by stealing from me. He was caught in the act of attempting to sell them in London. This put a damper on the day to start with, but the unpleasantness was soon forgotten as the day progressed.

I was allowed one guest, and I decided to ask Steve Diamond to accompany me; he accepted. I was toying with the idea of asking Janette, but I don't think her boyfriend would have appreciated it – especially as it involved staying in a posh hotel overnight.

The journey, taxi fares and accommodation were all financed by the Celebrities Guild, and I would like to take this opportunity of thanking the patrons, trustees and all the Guilders for making this one of the most memorable evenings I have ever spent in my life.

Steve and I arrived in our room at the hotel. My God, it was posh – bathrooms, showers and toilets en suite! We changed into our dinner suits (hired, of course) and headed towards the lift, which transported us to the dining room in which the awards were to be presented. God, what a reception – people applauding and shaking my hand, and cameras flashing! I recognised some of the people who were applauding: Cliff Morgan, Welsh rugby international (he was to be my 'minder'); Frankie Vaughan; Virginia McKenna of *Born Free* fame; Mo and Dr Legg from *Eastenders*; Lee Montague; Brian Johnson; Ruth Madoc of *Hi-Di-Hi* fame (she is as gorgeous in real life as she is on-screen); and many, many others.

We were seated eight to a table for the meal. By this time I was so excited. There were about five sets of forks, knives and spoons. 'God Almighty!' I thought. 'What bloody knives and forks do I use and in what sequence! Calm down, calm down!' I thought.

I vaguely remember someone telling me to start on the outside and work my way inwards with each course. I recognised a fish knife – all was not lost. 'Anyway,' I thought, 'I'll keep my eye on Cliff Morgan. He'll know what he's doing.' I thought, fleetingly, 'Whoever would have thought that old Special-Needs Hall would be sitting in a posh hotel dining with all these celebrities. God, what a feeling! What a thrill this was!

I cannot recall much about the meal – I was far too excited. I do remember afterwards, though, having great difficulty finding the loo – and who should be standing next to me but Frankie Vaughan. I guess I can now say in all honesty I've hung out with Frankie Vaughan. We discussed my efforts in the various marathons and what my plans were for the future. He showed great interest in me, congratulated me on receiving the award and wished me the best of luck.

Prior to the presentation, Cliff Morgan made a speech regarding why I was being given the award. He seemed to speak for ages about my disabilities, what I had achieved, the money I had raised, and so on. Eventually he asked me to step on to the stage to receive the award.

The applause was deafening. Everyone in the room stood as one, cheering and applauding.

"Well done! Well done! Bravo, bravo, John! Well done! Good on yer! Well done!"

At last the applause calmed down. I received the award and Cliff asked if I would like to say a few words.

I vaguely remember talking about my ambition to run from John o'Groats to Land's End for charity and thanking the Celebrities Guild from the bottom of my heart for their kindness and all that they do for charity. Of course I mentioned my good friends and the people of Ludgershall who had sponsored me and encouraged me from the start. The applause started again and went on for quite some time.

I have never felt more alive and wonderful than I did during that time.

I keep my award in a glass cabinet, and if ever I feel a bit down or slightly depressed I look at it and all the wonderful memories come flooding back; I soon feel much better.

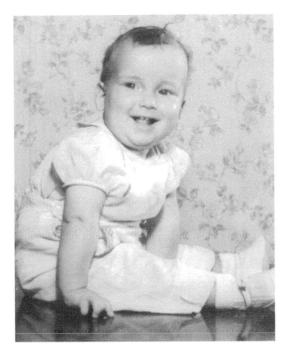

John, aged about one year.

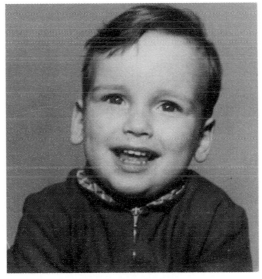

John, aged seven.

John's mother, June.

The grave of John's father in Trinidad.

Joe, June and John.

John and Janette.

Rayners School.

John in the Boeing 747 en route to New York.

New York.

John in the Olympic Stadium, Berlin.

John at Checkpoint Charlie.

John at the Berlin Wall.

ANDOVER ADVERTISER

DISTRICT NEWS

Local hero faces toughest challenge

Special Report by Deborah Courtnell

MARATHON man and local hero are two of the many labels that John Hall of Old Common Way, Ludgershall, has been given, but his most exciting venture to date could make him a celebrity in his own right, under his own name.

He entered his first marathon as a disabled runner in London, 1985. The following year he not only completed the New York marathon but bettered his own time. In 1987 he ran in Berlin and astounded people with a time a four hours 42 minutes, his personal best.

"Everytime I go to a big race I make sure I overcome my own world record. Nobody knows what my next time will be until I come to a halt."

The extraordinary determination which propels John Hall has rooted in 34 years of struggling to overcome the handicaps with which he was born.

"I am two people in one. When I'm not doing anything I'm a disabled man, when I'm running I'm John Hall. I say to myself 'Go on John, show them what you can do'."

There is a light in this man's eyes which masks any bitterness he may feel at his lot. He considers himself to

have been blessed with love throughout his life. His mother was a constant source of inspiration to him and her death from cancer, less than two years ago, left a gaping hole in his life.

It is in her honour that John is undertaking his next London marathon in April this year. And his supreme goal is dedicated to her memory: "My aim is to try to become the first disabled person to complete the John O'Groats to Lands End distance, and to enter the Guinness Book of Records."

Twisted

For the man who was born deaf, unable to speak, with twisted shoulders and 'legs bent like a banana' the catalogue of John's achievements and his bold eloquence are awesome.

His own hero is Sebastian Coe: "Most athletes don't have the courage to go out and give what

people demand. Coe has had the courage to come back and surpass himself, despite injuries. And I have the willpower to go on and become the runner which no-one thinks I can be," he declared.

Like Coe, patron of Motivor, the Motor Neurone disease charity, John Hall has devoted himself to fund-raising and has already donated nearly £4,000. He is running for Muscular Dystrophy in April.

"Fund-raising means a hell of a lot to me. The government can only do so much. It is up to disabled people to do the rest."

John's ambitions are unlimited. Ultimately he would like to devote himself full-time to fund-raising, creating a 'bank of funds as long-term, interest-earning security for charities.

The Armoured Vehicle Sub-Depot in Ludgershall where John has worked for 16 years and reached the position of storekeeper have pledged Army back-up for his 1991 John O'Groats challenge.

Anyone who would like to sponsor John in either of his forthcoming challenges should contact him at 5 Old Common Way, Ludgershall.

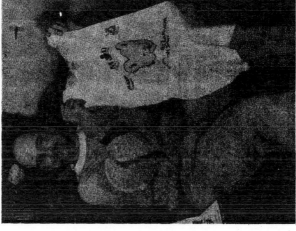

Marathon man John Hall.

9051-M7

Photograph by Caroline Mumford

105

THE CELEBRITIES GUILD OF GREAT BRITAIN

has pleasure in inviting

MR JOHN HALL

to the

Eighth Presentation of

CELEBRITIES GUILD
UNSUNG HEROES AWARDS

GALA EVENING

at the Royal Garden Hotel, High Street Kensington, London W8

SUNDAY NOVEMBER 4, 1990

6pm – 1am

Dancing to Ken Mackintosh and His Orchestra

Ticket £55
including

Reception • Dining • Wining • Presentation & Tributes • Midnight Tea • Dancing

Proceeds in aid of
Lambeth Community Care Centre
and
Camphill Village Trust Homes for the Mentally Handicapped

ADMISSION STRICTLY BY THIS TICKET ONLY

Black Tie

COMPLIMENTARY

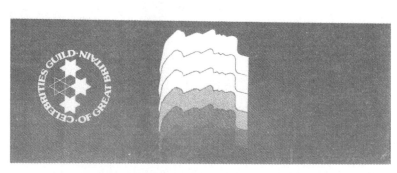

An invitation from the Celebrities Guild.

FOUNDER: ELLA GLAZER

EG/EH/IH90

14 EAST BARNET ROAD
NEW BARNET
HERTS EN4 8RW

Telephone: 081-449 1234
081-449 1515 081-441 2122
(10am-4pm, Weekdays)

October 25, 1990

Mr. J.P.M. Hall
10 Old Common Way,
Ludgershall,
nr. Andover,
Hampshire,
SP11 9RX

Dear Mr. Hall,

This is just to let you have final details with regard to our Gala Evening on Sunday, November 4.

We have booked accommodation for you and Jeanette Slaven to stay at the Royal Horseguards Thistle Hotel, Whitehall Court, London SW1 (telephone 071 839 3400). Once you have settled into your hotel in the afternoon of Sunday week, please could you be waiting at the Reception Desk in the foyer no later than 5.15 pm.

At that time, Alma Golding, who is the Treasurer of our GUILD and one of the people helping to organise this event, will be there to arrange for you to go in a taxi to the Royal Garden Hotel in Kensington for the evening's events. At that hotel you will be met by Lee Montague one of the members of our Organising Committee, who will 'keep an eye on you' for the entire evening in case there is anything you need.

I understand that Frieda Gunn (who is coming with her Husband) prefers not to stay overnight, but they will be going direct to the Royal Garden Hotel in time for the start of our Gala Evening.

You will be returned to the Royal Horseguards Hotel at 1 am on November 5.

We do hope that all these arrangements are satisfactory and look forward to seeing you.

All good wishes.

Yours sincerely,

Ella Glazer (Mrs)
Hon. Exec. Guilder

P.S. Could you kindly give all this information to Mrs. Gunn

Charity Reg. No. 282298

A letter from the Celebrities Guild.

107

John with Mr and Mrs Gumm,
who nominated him for the Unsung Heroes award.

Cliff Morgan and John.

One of the most memorable evenings of John's life . . .

. . . the Unsung Heroes awards ceremony.

EG/JA/UH90

14 EAST BARNET ROAD
NEW BARNET
HERTS EN4 8RW

Telephone: 081-449 1234
081-449 1515 081-441 2122
(10am-4pm, Weekdays)

7 November 1990

Mr J Hall
10 Old Common Way
Ludgershall
Nr Andover
Hants
SP11 9RX

Dear John,

This is just to let you have some photos of our 'Do' on Sunday.

It was lovely to meet you and we do hope you will keep in touch.

Warmest good wishes from us all at the CELEBRITIES GUILD.

Yours very sincerely,

Ella Glazer (Mrs)
Hon. Exec. Guilder

Enc.

Warmest wishes from the Celebrities Guild.

110

Unsung hero John to collect his award

A 34-YEAR-OLD handicapped man, who has raised thousands of pounds for the disabled by running in marathons, is to receive an Unsung Hero award in London next month.

The Celebrities Guild, which makes the annual awards, says that John Hall, of Old Common Way, Ludgershall, near Andover, "displays self-effacing determination, outstanding courage in the face of great adversity and has a warm interest in those worse off than himself."

John, a storeman at the Army's vehicle depot in Ludgershall, has run in four marathons — London twice, Berlin and New York — and he hopes to take part in the London event again next year.

But he has had to overcome physical handicaps faced by few if any of the competitors in these events.

John is, in fact, a spastic. He was born with a twisted leg, deaf and with difficulty in speaking.

Report by John Anderson

He has conquered his deafness, overcome his speech impediment, helped others to master sign language and learned to walk. But, he says: "I can run better than I can walk."

John, who is delighted with the award which will be presented to him at a London hotel on November 4, has raised £5,000 to the help disabled in the last few years. "I couldn't have done it without the help of the people of Ludgershall."

He has lived alone since his mother died five years ago. "Every time I run I think of my mum." he says.

Life has been a tough, uphill struggle for John who first started running when he was 26 and weighing a thumping 17 stones. "I could hardly walk never mind run."

He slimmed down to 11 stone and took part in his first half marathon in 1983, finishing last with bleeding thighs and feet. Undeterred, he ran in first the London and then the New York and Berlin marathons completing the course each time.

John's ambition is to become a full-time fundraiser to help handicapped people and the charities which care for them. He has gone back to school to improve his reading, writing and spelling "so that I can then go to college and get some qualifications. I would really like to work in a large organisation helping disabled people."

AWARD: Marathon runner John Hall.

John and Mandy's home in Canada.

John and Mandy.

CHAPTER XIV

THE 1992 POOLE MARATHON

I decided to have a rest from running for a while, but this decision was short-lived. The work project for the deaf at Enham Alamein, near Andover, required funds, and at a meeting with their committee it was agreed that, providing we could acquire sponsors, I would attempt to run from John o'Groats to Land's End. It was also agreed that the committee at Enham Alamein and I would work together regarding the organisation of transport, accommodation, route and, most importantly, sponsorship.

Unfortunately this project did not even get off the ground. I had to obtain leave from the officer in charge of the Central Vehicle Depot, and unfortunately they couldn't spare me for the time I would need to be away. My services were required kitting out Challengers, Warriors and Saxons as well as working on various missiles. They were required for the Gulf War, which had reared its ugly head. The John o'Groats run, therefore, was postponed.

As things in the Gulf began to stabilise, I had the urge to run again. I decided to have a crack at the Poole Marathon, and I applied through *Marathon Magazine*. I did not have time to organise any sponsorship for this one. Instead I treated it as a 'getting fit and keeping fit' exercise.

It was a good experience as far as I was concerned. I had to organise bed-and-breakfast accommodation. I remember it was a very clean, comfortable guesthouse and cost £35 per night, including evening meal. That, I thought, was pretty fair.

I arrived on 6 June, the day before the marathon, and in the early evening I decided to do a bit of light jogging, get back for my evening meal, have a nice hot bath and settle down for a rest. God, wasn't I getting sensible!

On the day of the race I rose fairly early and ate a light breakfast, then packed my bag and headed towards Tower Park, where the marathon was to start. I had asked someone to look after my gear for me. The familiar sequence of events unfolded: the banter with other runners, the joking and the laughing, the general mickey-taking.

The start gun fired. We were off!

There were not as many runners in this marathon as I had become used to so the field seemed to thin out rather quickly as the faster runners shot ahead. Something I had not bargained for was the terrain – the hills and valleys. I was used to running on the flat.

'Ah well, plod on, John, plod on,' I thought.

I passed various markers and the dreaded 'sweaty-feet syndrome' began to take hold. First my feet start to itch, then they feel red-hot, then the sweat starts to ooze between my toes. I knew I was going to be in for a rough time. I decided to run barefoot for a while. This didn't help at all – in fact, it made things worse. On, on I went. After I had passed the same marker two or three times, I realised I had been running in circles.

A car pulled up alongside. I think they thought I was dropping out.

I told them, "No, no, I am just lost. For God's sake show me the way out of here."

A marshal who should have been at a certain point to indicate the route thought that an eighty-five-year-old man was the last competitor, and he had left his marker point. Consequently yours truly had run an extra five miles!

The way home was along a beach. Have you ever run on sand? My legs felt as though they belonged to someone else at this stage. I have never been closer to giving up.

'What the hell!' I thought. 'I won't be letting any sponsors down.' – I didn't have any. 'Hang on, hang on,' I thought, 'what about me? I will be letting myself down. Two miles to go – just two miles! Keep going, keep going. Imagine being beaten by an eighty-five-year-old man. Ah well,' I thought, 'I have run five more bloody miles than he has.'

The radio commentator mentioned that I was to receive a consolation prize – a model owl. Oh well, that was quite appropriate. By this time I didn't give two hoots anyway.

I received my medal for completing the course, but this time there was no gorgeous dolly bird; she had probably gone home.

No, the Poole Marathon does not hold the happiest memories.

What I do recall is a Japanese tourist at the first-aid point taking photographs of me having my feet treated by paramedics. I guess that somewhere in Japan there must be photographs of my blistered 'bats' in several photograph albums.

That evening I was standing at the bar having a drink before dinner. Two or three old dears were discussing the marathon, and in particular this poor chap who had staggered in and had been assisted to the first-aid post with red-raw, bleeding feet.

They were utterly amazed when the proprietor pointed out to them that I, in fact, was one and the same person. I spent the next half an hour or so being mollycoddled and signing autographs. A pleasant evening was spent by all. Then I went upstairs and packed, ready for my return journey to Ludgershall.

CHAPTER XV

MANDY

I had been suffering a great deal with back problems, and in 1993 I decided to have a rest from running for a while to try to cure this niggling problem.

During this time I did most of my shopping in the Gateway Supermarket. Imagine my surprise when I went to buy my tins of soup (all I could afford) and realised the checkout assistant was Mandy, a girl I had previously encountered at the Central Vehicle Depot, where she was employed as a cleaner.

The Vehicle Depot Dance was looming, and I thought about asking Mandy if she would care to partner me. I knew she had been married but that her husband and she had decided to separate. Yes, I had done my homework. With all this in mind and the approval of my friend Janette, whose opinion I valued, I decided to ask Mandy to join me. Mandy wasn't sure, but I gave her the ticket in any case and told her if she changed her mind just to come along. She offered to pay for the ticket and said that she might come. She wasn't sure.

The night of the ball arrived, and, as I was not really expecting Mandy to turn up, I became involved in one of the organised activities. I think it was a treasure hunt. Suddenly one of my friends came up to me and informed me that there was a young lady at the gate looking for John Hall. It was Mandy.

I was more than surprised that Mandy had turned up, but, without further ado, I ran down to the gate and apologised for not being there to greet her. I explained that I had not really thought she was all that keen on coming to the dance.

I do not remember very much of the evening. From then on I was in a bit of a dream, but I do remember being very proud of the fact that Mandy was there with me. We danced the night away, and I remember thinking and feeling that I could get quite serious about this young lady.

The dance finished about 2 a.m., and Mandy offered to drive me home. I invited her in for coffee, but she declined as it was so late. I was very disappointed; I did not want the evening to end.

The following day I had arranged to babysit for Janette. Mandy tried to contact me, but of course I was not at home to answer her call.

The following day when I arrived home, the telephone was ringing. I thought it was a female insurance agent I had contacted regarding a policy, so I invited her along to discuss insurance. Mandy played along. Imagine my surprise when the doorbell rang and I opened the door to find Mandy standing there. I invited Mandy in and made coffee. We sat chatting for ages and agreed that it would be nice to go out together as friends and see how the relationship developed.

The months seemed to fly past and, as I had hoped, the relationship became more serious. Mandy's divorce was finalised, and we both considered ourselves a couple. We had long, serious discussions regarding our future.

Mandy had been married to an army chap and had lived in married quarters, which now she had to vacate as soon as possible. This did not present too much of a problem as I was currently living in a two-bedroom house at 10 Old Common Way. I invited Mandy and her two children to live with me until we decided what best to do for the future.

Oh, the sheer joy of having someone to share my life with! Here I was with a lovely young lady living under the same roof, and two children to consider – a vast difference from the somewhat self-centred existence I had been used to.

I had been suffering from a chest infection for quite some time, and Mandy had been doing her Florence Nightingale impression. One day she was rather concerned. I was a bit red in the face and sweating like a pig. She sent for the doctor. My temperature was way above what it should have been. The doctor pulled back the bedclothes to have a listen to my chest.

"Good God!" he exclaimed, "If you removed your dressing gown and the jersey you've got on, your temperature should drop immediately."

Mandy was killing herself laughing. She hadn't realised I had been wearing all this clobber. She laughed and laughed; the tears were rolling down her cheeks.

Without thinking, I proposed that we become engaged. That stopped her in her tracks. She became very serious, looked me straight in the eye and, to my great joy, accepted my proposal.

This was beyond my wildest dreams. At last, not only could I visualise a family of my own, but also, if everything went according to plan, it would become reality.

We planned an engagement party at the Vehicle Depot Club and made the decision to work and save for about two years. This would allow us to get to know each other better, and also, of course, there were Mandy's two children to consider. Not least of all, it was going to cost for a wedding and a honeymoon, and I had not been the most frugal person.

Two years flew past and we tried for a larger house – one with another bedroom. The children were growing fast and would need a bedroom each – their own space. We were fortunate and moved into 37 Perham Crescent, Ludgershall. We settled into our new life very quickly, and we commenced to plan the wedding and the honeymoon. Meanwhile Mandy was also working all hours that God gave to enable us to achieve our goals – part-time in Gateways, cleaning and babysitting were some of the many occupations she was involved in. We both realised that on my salary alone it would take for ever.

The wedding was set for 6 May 1994 at the Andover Registry Office, then the next day, for the church blessing and the reception. The reception was to be held in the Andover Football Club.

Saturday 7 May 1994 was the most fantastic, fabulous, proudest day of my entire life.

The following Wednesday we flew from Gatwick Airport to Cyprus for our honeymoon, having previously booked self-catering accommodation in Limassol. The children stayed with Mandy's parents.

I don't really remember much about the flight. As you can imagine, I was so excited by the whole procedure. I do remember arriving at our flat to a wonderful welcome.

There was a bouquet of flowers for Mandy and a welcoming bottle of champagne on ice, and to my amazement there was also a birthday card. I guess Mandy must have organised that. I reckon this was the happiest birthday of my life.

The most miserable part of our honeymoon was a trip to Egypt to see the Pyramids. There is little wonder that the Sphinx has a permanent inscrutable smile on its face, witnessing all the sweaty, ill-tempered British tourists being hustled along like demented cattle by an equally ill-tempered tour guide.

"Hurry, hurry, we must hurry!" was the cry.

God, we were pleased to get back to the smelly, hot, humid boat that was to transport us back to Cyprus.

This experience was soon forgotten, though, when my wife (sounds good, eh!) hired a car for a couple of days and drove us all over Cyprus.

Another incident that springs to mind was— the hotel caught fire! I was in the bath enjoying a good old soak when suddenly Mandy came rushing in.

"John, John, the hotel's on fire."

Bells were ringing, staff were panicking, fire engines were arriving and the place started to fill with smoke. They found that a chip pan had caught fire in the kitchen and quickly dealt with it. I continued with my bath and got ready for the evening's entertainment.

The rest of the holiday passed very quickly – beautiful sunshine, swimming, going for drives, going out for dinner, a few drinks, a lovely wife. God, this is the life! But all good things come to an end – especially those that you wish could last for ever. Soon we were both thinking about home and what that was going to entail – certainly a whole new ball game, as far as I was concerned. I must admit I was a wee bit apprehensive. There were two children to think about. Would I cope? Would I be a good husband? All of these thoughts and doubts crossed my mind, but, as with marathon-running, one must approach life with a positive attitude. I was determined to make our marriage work, and up to then we were doing fine.

Quite a bit happened since our marriage. I was made redundant from the Central Vehicle Depot, but I managed to find employment with the Medical Supplies Agency in Ludgershall. Mandy was still slaving away at several jobs, and we bought a new house – 39 Linden Close, Ludgershall, where we gradually got it together.

CHAPTER XVI

CANADA

Mandy's parents lived in Shropshire, so they did not visit us very often. On one occasion when they did visit, they hinted that they planned to emigrate to Canada. This upset Mandy; she did not want them to go. It became obvious that Mandy's parents were determined to proceed with their plans; and without my knowledge they decided that Mandy, the children and I should eventually join them.

One day, after Mandy's parents and her brother had emigrated to Canada, Mandy said that she would like to visit them. By this time they were settled in. I knew Mandy was missing them, so I agreed to join her for a holiday. Of course at this time I was completely in the dark regarding her parents' real intentions.

We were greeted at the airport in Toronto by my father-in-law, and we continued by car to Hanover. The whole journey took about twelve hours. This part of Canada was not what I had imagined in my mind's eye (that is, mountains, flowing rivers, waterfalls, etc.); it was very flat. I immediately thought, 'I wouldn't like to live here,' still unaware that it was the ultimate intention of the family that we should also emigrate and live with them as one family under one roof.

The fortnight passed very quickly and, I must say, I did enjoy it. When we left I was still blissfully unaware of the scheming that had gone on behind my back, including the fact that the sale of our house in Ludgershall was planned in order to help to finance the 'Canadian dream'.

We arrived back home and I returned to work with the MOD only to find that they had decided to retire me on medical grounds due to a back injury that had occurred at work several weeks earlier. Fortunately I was granted a full MOD pension, as well as a gratuity which balanced out the Canadian holiday expenses.

Mandy was obviously not happy. She complained bitterly about missing her parents. Our marriage began to deteriorate. Mandy seemed to be losing interest, and this led to more bickering, heated discussions and arguments. Mandy's pleading won in the end. I just couldn't stand it any more. She wore me down like the sea gradually wearing away at the shore. I agreed to attend an emigration medical, but I secretly hoped that I would fail, and that therefore we would have to stay at home. Unfortunately, I passed the medical, and I agreed to emigrate.

On the day I made the decision, exactly half an hour later, a woman arrived on the doorstep with a view to buying the house. Mandy, however, said she knew nothing of this.

The sale of the house, fixtures and fittings all went smoothly. I was not really a very happy chappie, but I wanted my marriage to work so I was considering my wife's wishes.

We now started looking for accommodation in Canada. I thought a bungalow (all on one level) would be ideal, but the clan had other ideas. They had their eye on a farmhouse with one and a half acres of ground, so that we could all live together and become, as far as possible, self-sufficient. I felt this would be a recipe for disaster, but I had already given Mandy full control of our family finances. It is truly amazing how being in love (which I was) clouds one's judgement.

As time went by I became more and more unhappy. I felt like a complete outsider, never being included in any discussions regarding the property. Mandy's father was top dog, making most, if not all, the decisions. During this time I felt I had to try to nurture other interests outside the family circle, so I joined the Salvation Army. I made some wonderful friends, and it gave me something to look forward to away from family problems.

I remained in Canada for a further two years, hoping that life would improve, but it became apparent that my marriage was over. The realisation that everything had been planned without any consideration for me was devastating.

Mandy's father was also involved in the Salvation Army. In fact, I think it was he who persuaded me to join. Most of the members knew the family, and it was at a Salvation Army get-together that a fellow member drew me aside and informed me he had been to a concert and witnessed Mandy and another man in a pretty serious clinch, kissing. He said it was obviously not a friendly peck on the cheek! I was absolutely gutted.

I confronted Mandy, and she denied it, but I knew she was lying. It was becoming blatantly obvious that the family wanted me out of the way. Eventually during one of our many arguments she completely lost control and came out with the truth: she had married me for a bit of paper and all that went with it.

CHAPTER XVII

HOME AGAIN

I decided to phone my friends in Ludgershall, Tom and Maggie Blair, and I explained that Mandy had suggested that I came home for good. I asked them if they could pick us up at the airport. On two previous occasions they had given me sanctuary when I had been at a very low ebb and just had to come back home to recharge my batteries.

Mandy booked me a one-way ticket to England, and herself a return, having organised accommodation in Andover. She also contacted social services regarding where I was going to live. All I had at this stage was what was in my bags and the clothes I stood up in. Eventually I was placed in a home for the homeless in Devises, twenty miles away from my beloved Ludgershall and all my friends. When I thought of what I had before – my new home and a village full of friends – I just wept and became very depressed. In fact, I became quite ill. This lasted for about six months.

Social services were brilliant. They found me a flat in Ludgershall, where I wanted to be. It was a bit grotty, but my friends all rallied round and we soon had it spick and span. As usual I was bouncing back.

A few months passed and divorce papers arrived. I tried to persuade Mandy to reconsider, but to no avail. The truth was, I still loved her, but now I realised that the marriage had been a gigantic con. Eventually agreement was reached and the divorce became absolute.

About this time I got a job as a waiter in the army barracks, but unfortunately, because of my disability (my balance and deafness, etc.), I was getting the orders mixed up, dropping plates, tripping up and God knows what else. In the end they transferred me to a cleaning job, but the management soon realised that I wasn't cut out for that either. What they expected me to do in an hour took me a full day (even though I was trying my best), so they transferred me to the kitchens in Swinton Barracks. My new job was washing pots and general cleaning. During this time I was becoming quite unwell, and I really was not fit to work. The unfortunate outcome was that I was sacked.

I started to feel very ill indeed, and I made an appointment to see the doctor. Irritable bowel syndrome was diagnosed, but despite medication the pain became unbearable. This went on for a long time. I was in such pain one day that I contacted a friend and he agreed to take me to Salisbury District Hospital, where the Doctor immediately suggested I underwent a full body scan.

The following day I had an appointment with a specialist, and I was given the devastating news that I had cancer. Immediate surgery was advised. The diagnosis was a carcinoid tumour of the colon. A hemicolectomy was advised (that is, the diseased part of the colon would be removed).

I received a letter from Salisbury District Hospital asking me to attend on Sunday 3 April 2005, and to be prepared to undergo major surgery that week.

The surgery was successful as far as the colon was concerned, but unfortunately during surgery several tumours were discovered on my liver, and a further scan was arranged at Southampton University Hospital.

The scan took place at the beginning of June and it was recommended that Dr Iveson, the liver specialist, should continue to see me regularly during my follow-up procedures.

Further visits to Southampton University Hospital ensued, culminating in further scans, and on 31 January 2007 a letter arrived, informing me that the radiologist had found a few more tiny lesions. They suggested a procedure known as embolisation. (This is where they feed a very fine tube through the blood vessels from the top of the leg all the way up to the liver and then block off the blood supply to the tumour inside the liver using tiny spheres which clog up the capillaries to the tumour, starving it of blood.) This treatment of early tumours may in some cases make further surgical options less complicated.

Another letter, received on 28 February, informed me that I was to undergo the abovementioned treatment on 7 March with a follow-up scan on 20 March. Further appointments followed, the next being 3 May.

The embolisation of the recent lesions appeared to be successful, but I was informed that surgery would be necessary on the existing tumours. Another complete body scan was scheduled for 28 January 2008, and this indicated that further surgery was necessary. An appointment was made for a pre-op assessment on 11 June. Also scheduled was a cross-sectional liver scan. A liver resection for secondary liver cancer was recommended, and arrangements were made for an operation at Southampton University Hospital on 8 July, under the care of Mr N. Pearces.

I returned home after about five days, and, as you can imagine, I felt pretty rough.

Gradually I began to get my strength back. I have been told that there is no permanent cure, but I am being monitored by the surgical team.

I cannot thank the team enough. It really makes me angry when I hear people running down the NHS. Their professionalism, kindness and, above all, their honesty regarding my prognosis has been absolutely wonderful. Thank you all from the bottom of my heart.

I was subsequently given an appointment with a Dr D. J. Breen to be assessed regarding radio-frequency treatment. This took place on 3 November 2008, and was followed by more treatment on 10 November (radio-frequency ablation of two liver metastases, or small tumours). Since the radio-frequency treatment I have had a couple of scans, the last being on 16 November 2008.

This brings my story bang up to date. There are thousands of other cancer patients in the same boat. God bless all the surgeons, GPs, nurses and other staff who work endlessly for our benefit.

At the moment I am feeling so well that I have started a bit of light training and even tried a little gentle jogging. My one burning ambition still remains to attempt John o'Groats to Land's End for charity. Who knows? One day . . . Well, 'Never, never let go of your dreams' – this is my motto.

ACKNOWLEDGEMENTS

The surgeons and staff at Salisbury District Hospital;

The surgeons and staff at Southampton University Hospital;

Tom and Barbara Humphries, for their kindness and support;

Norman Stevens, for his friendship and support;

Bob Powell, for his friendship and support;

Janette Slaven, a lifelong friend;

Penn School, formerly Rayners School;

Collingbourne Harriers, for their patience and training;

Anne and Pete Mellors and Maggie Blair for their typing skills;

All of my friends, for their understanding and love;

The people of Ludgershall, for their ongoing support;

Last, but not least, my dear old friends Tom and Maggie Blair. Tom has listened patiently to my story throughout five and a half years, during our spare time, and who has transposed my verbal account into the written word.